[CHAPTER TWO]

I LOVE MY BOY

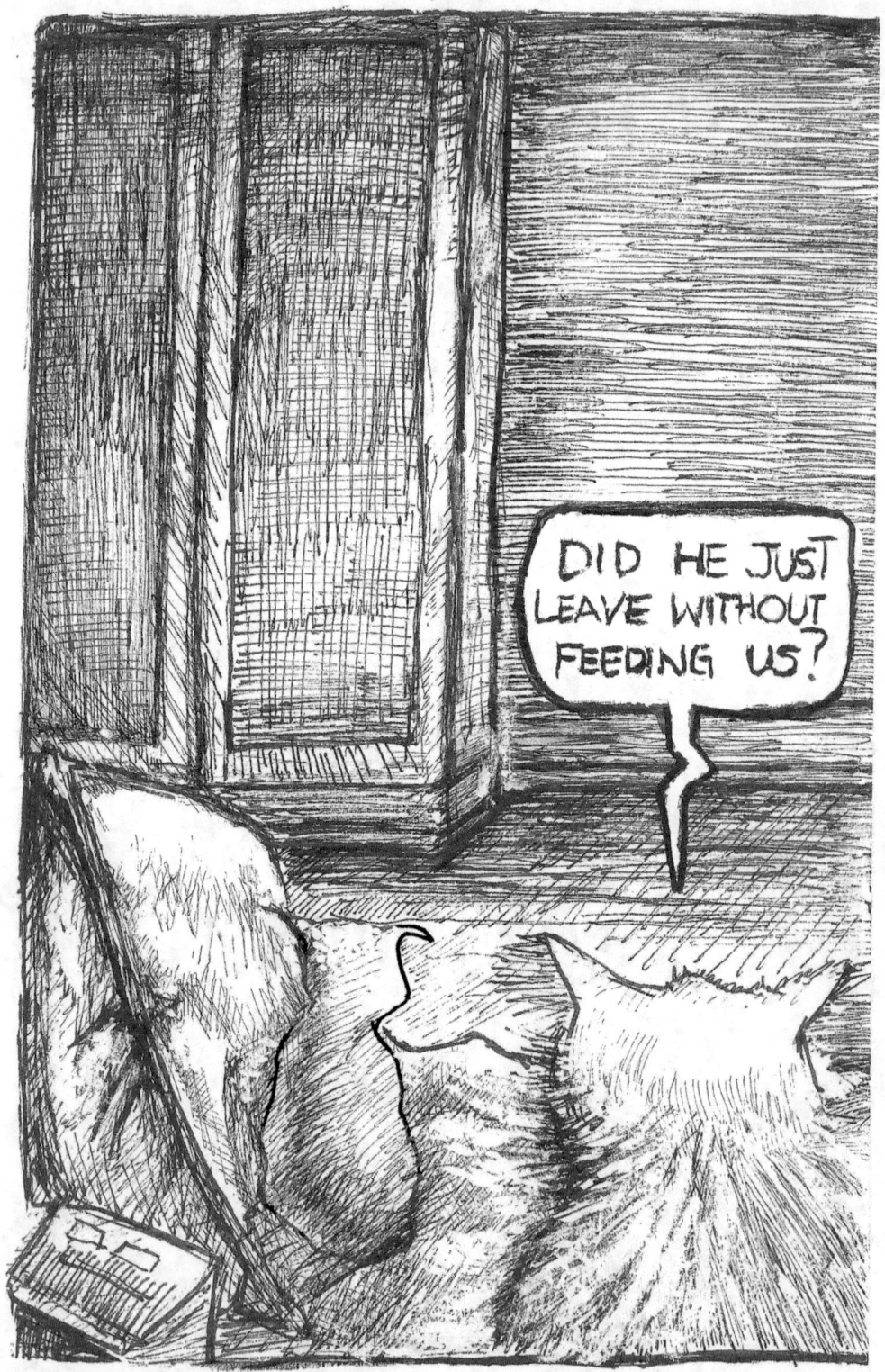

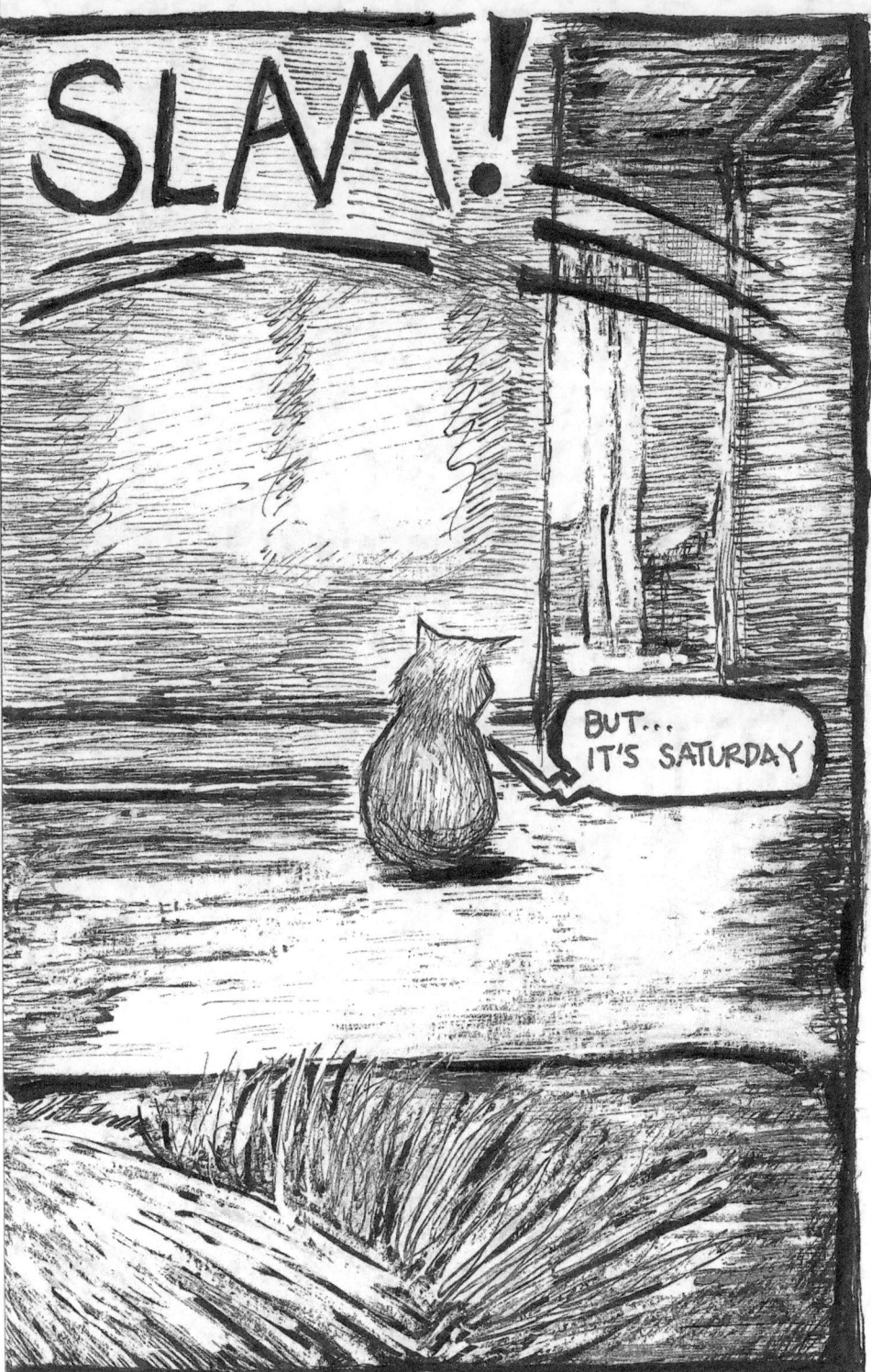

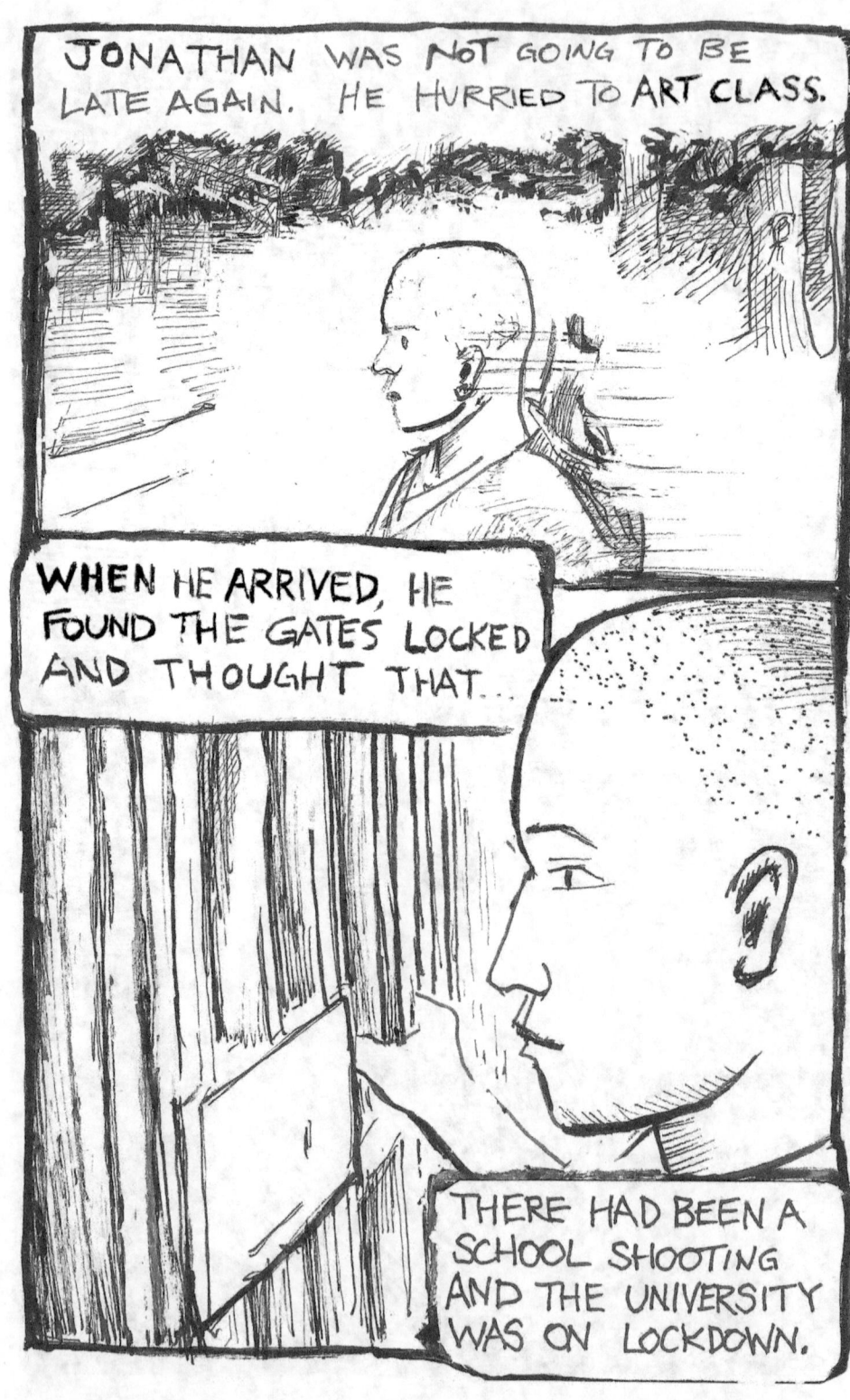

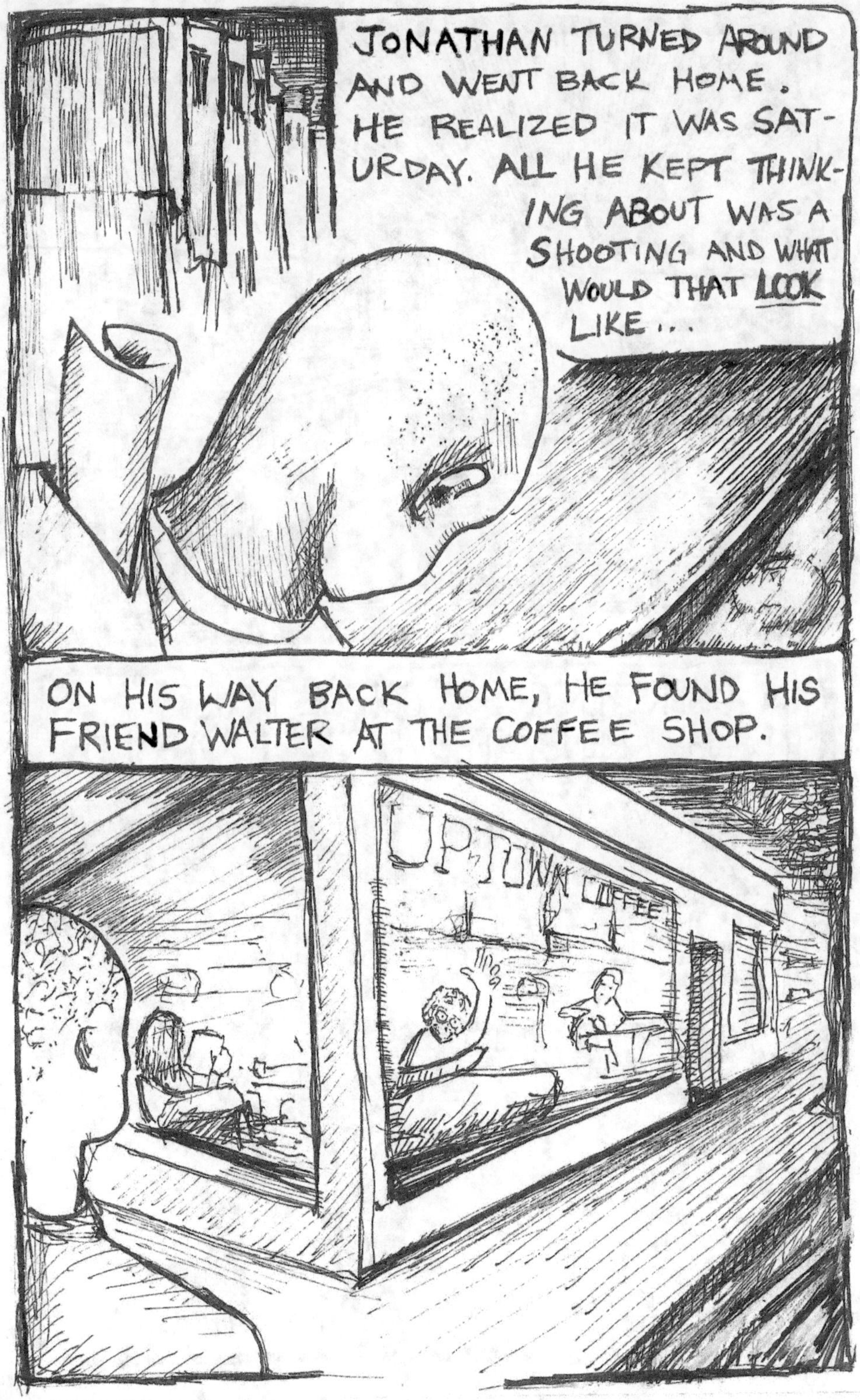

JONATHAN TURNED AROUND AND WENT BACK HOME. HE REALIZED IT WAS SATURDAY. ALL HE KEPT THINKING ABOUT WAS A SHOOTING AND WHAT WOULD THAT <u>LOOK</u> LIKE...

ON HIS WAY BACK HOME, HE FOUND HIS FRIEND WALTER AT THE COFFEE SHOP.

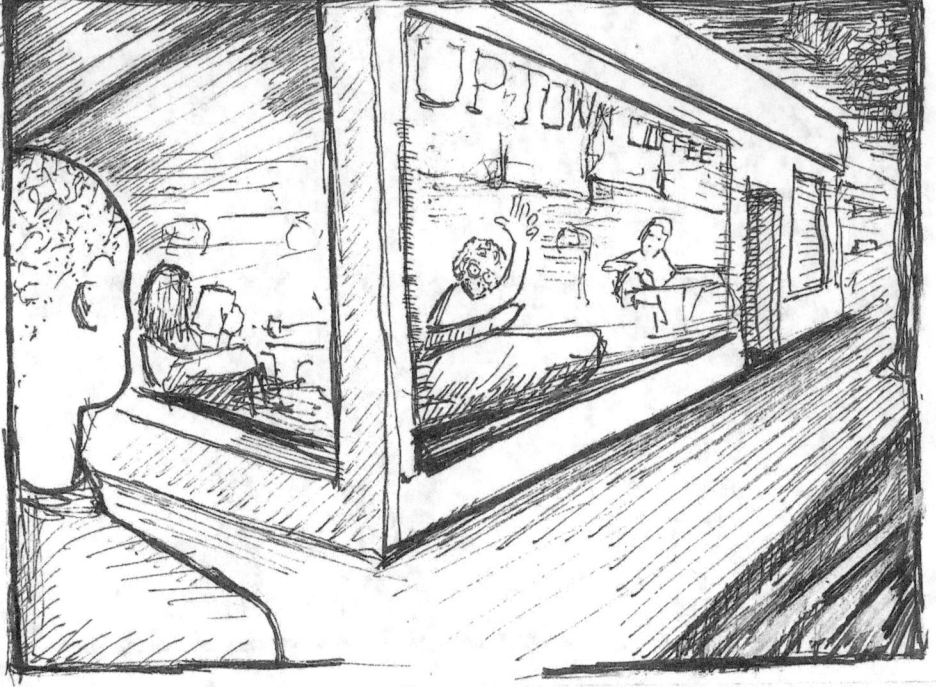

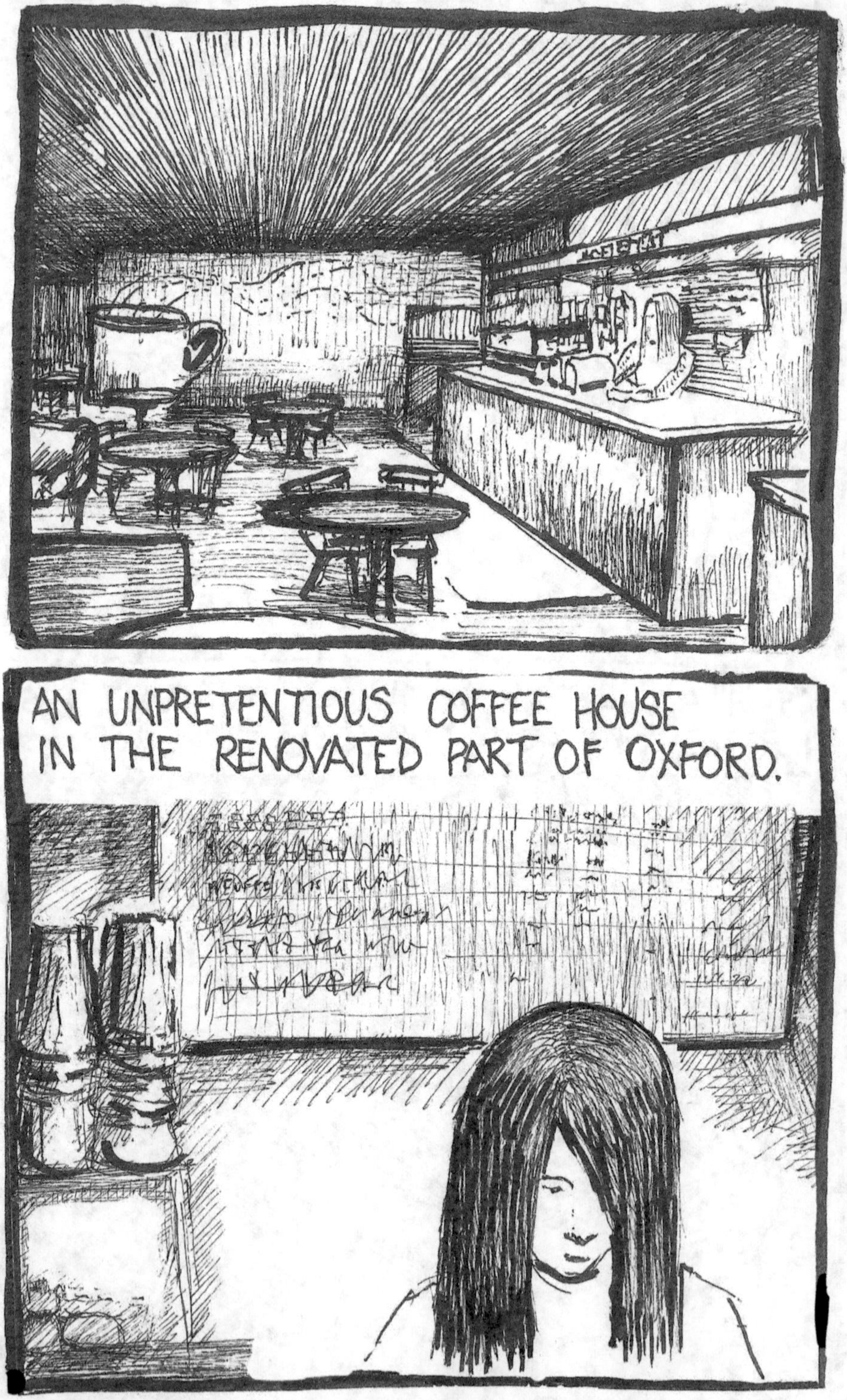

AN UNPRETENTIOUS COFFEE HOUSE IN THE RENOVATED PART OF OXFORD.

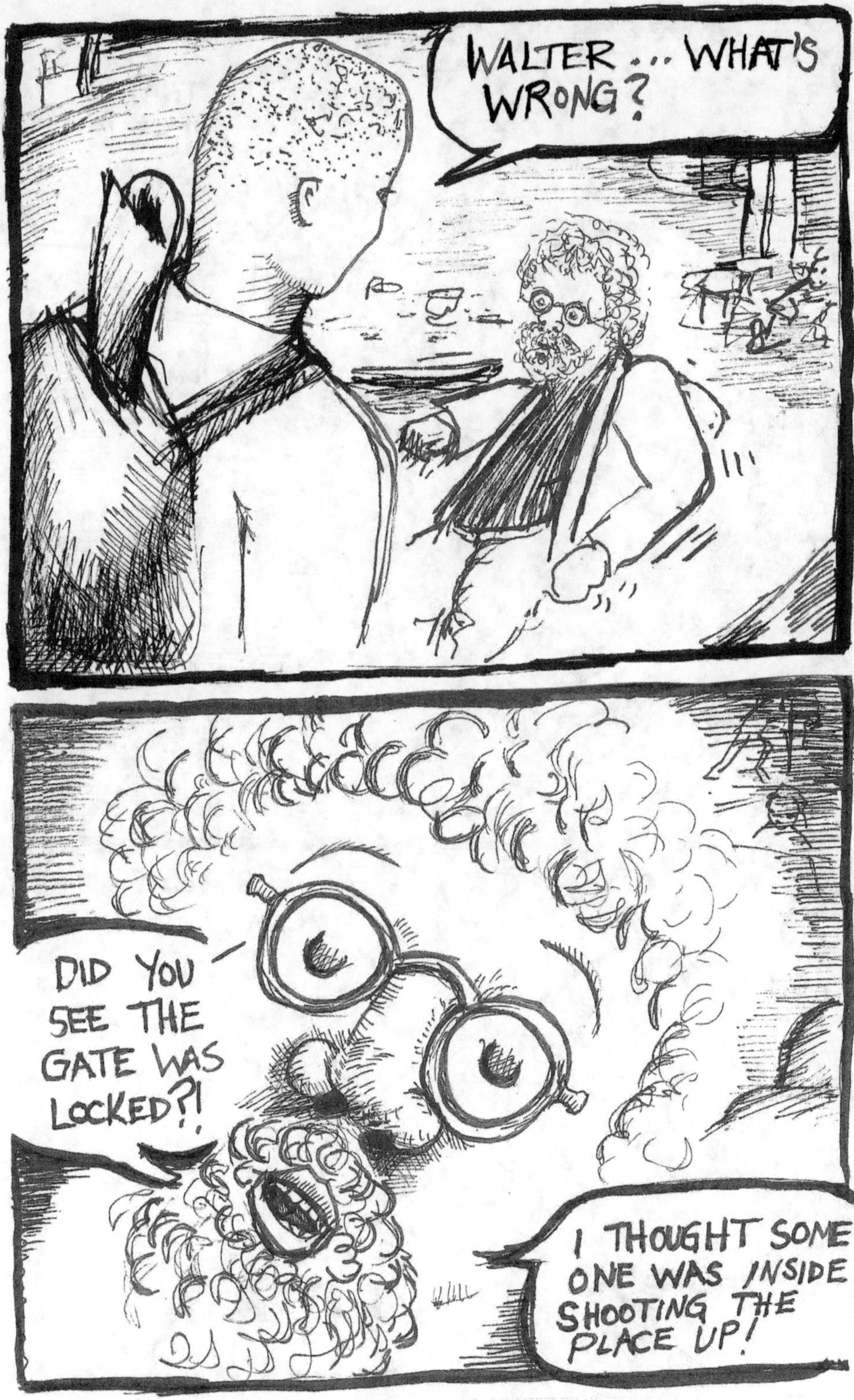
WALTER ... WHAT'S WRONG?
DID YOU SEE THE GATE WAS LOCKED?!
I THOUGHT SOME ONE WAS INSIDE SHOOTING THE PLACE UP!

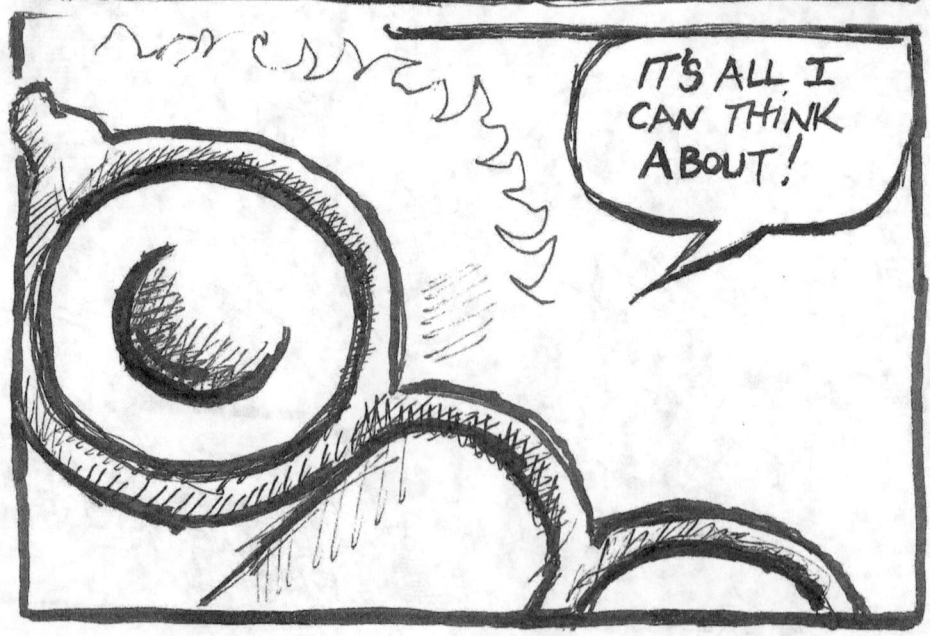

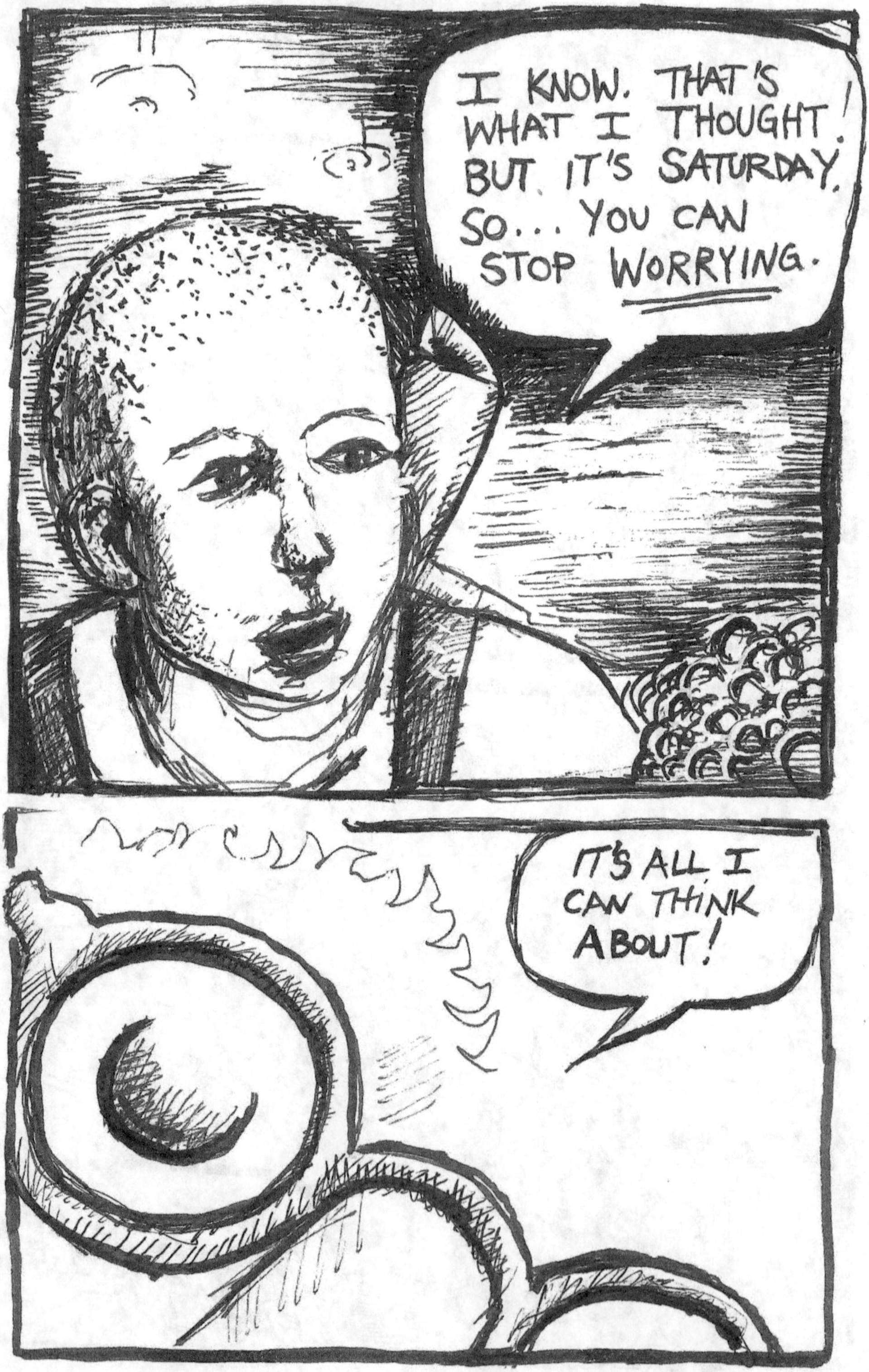

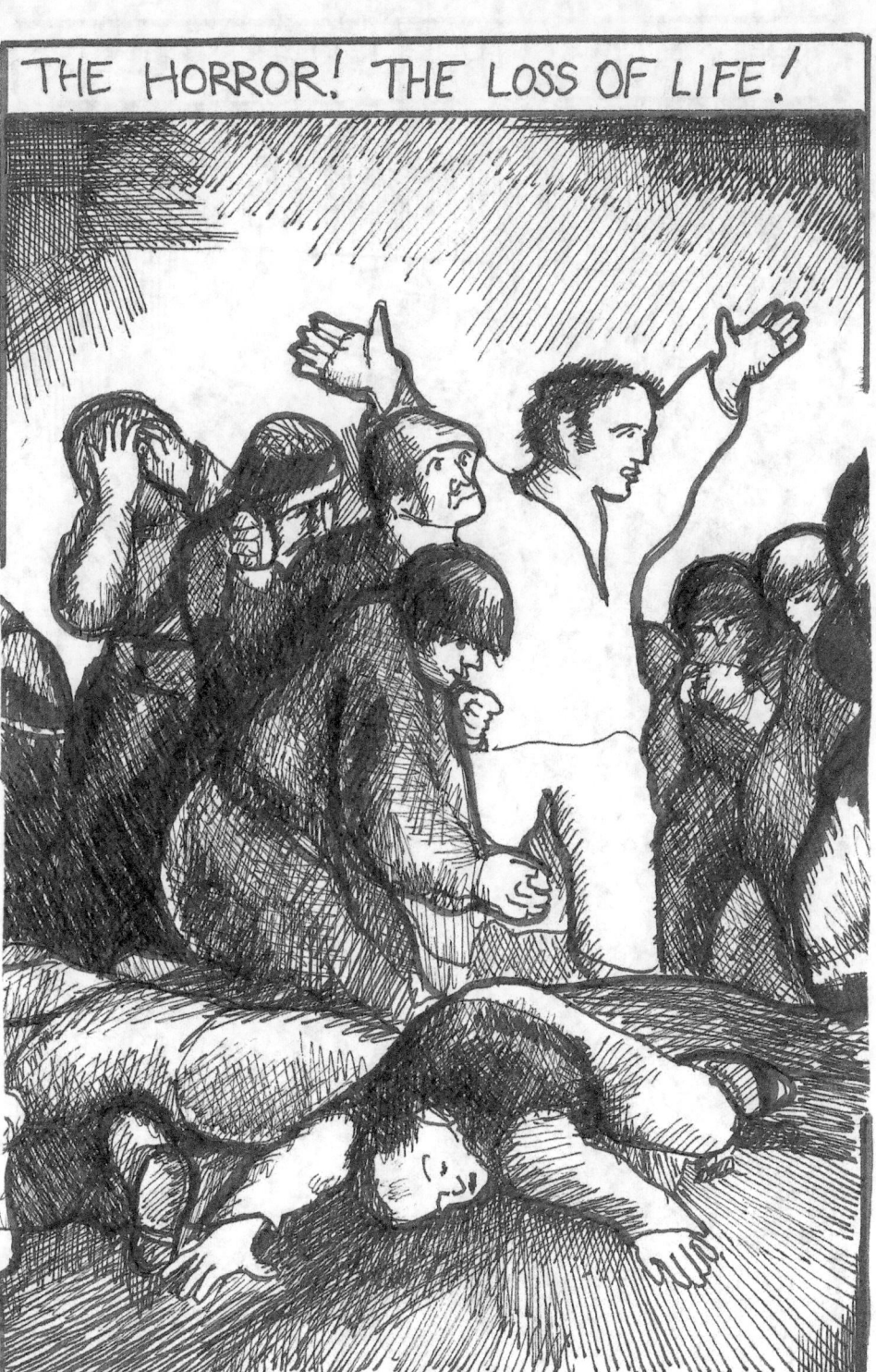

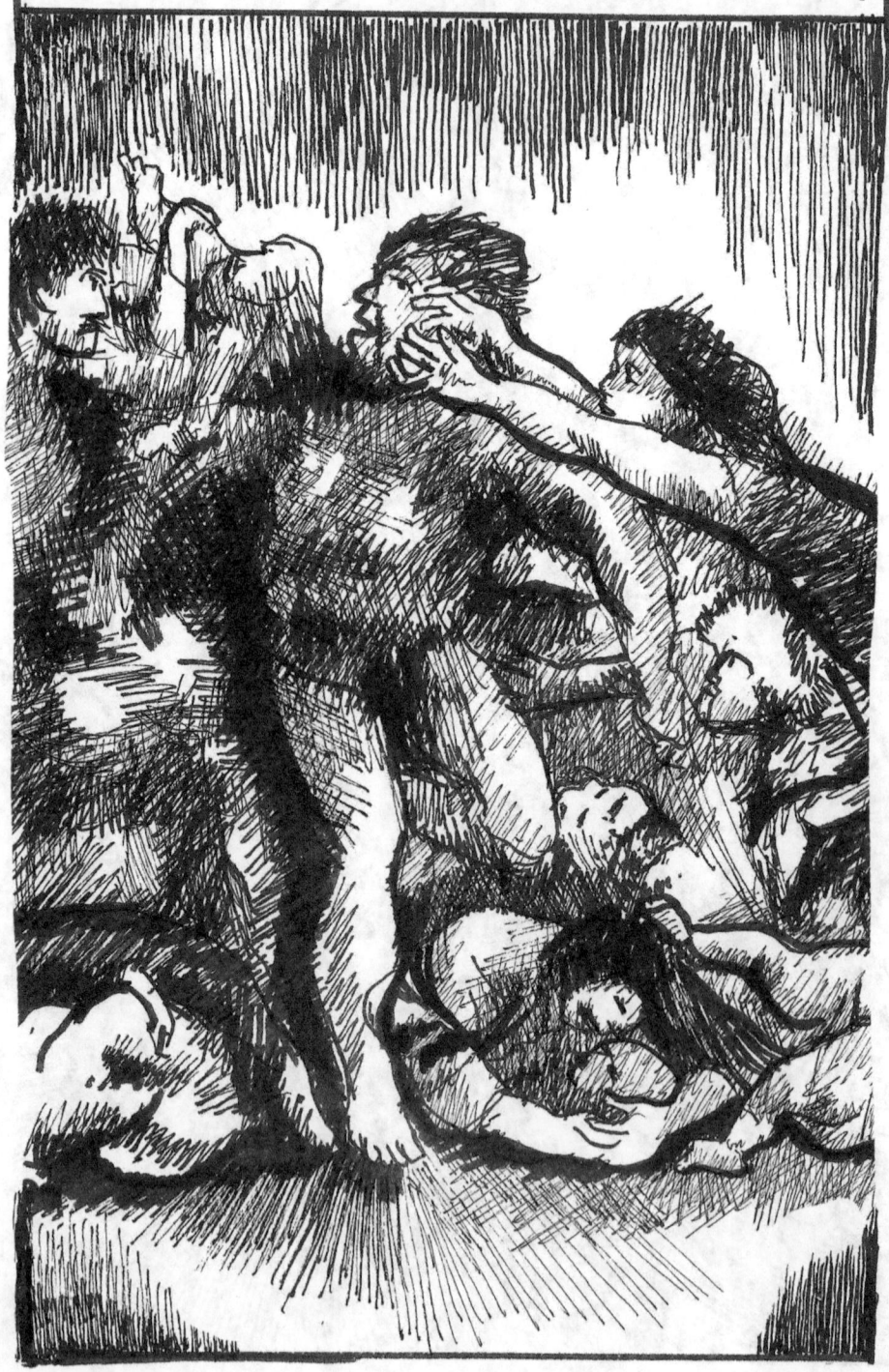

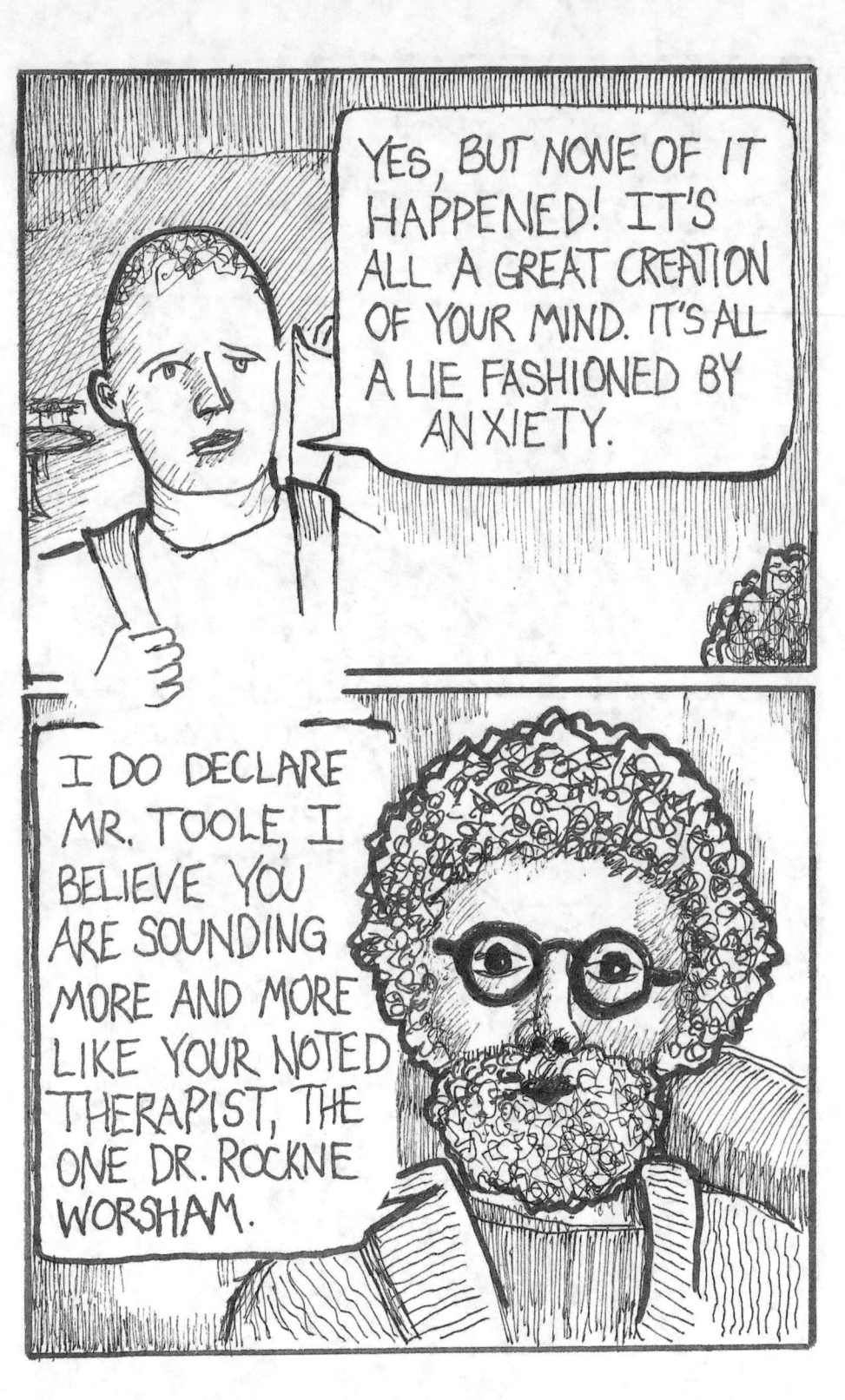

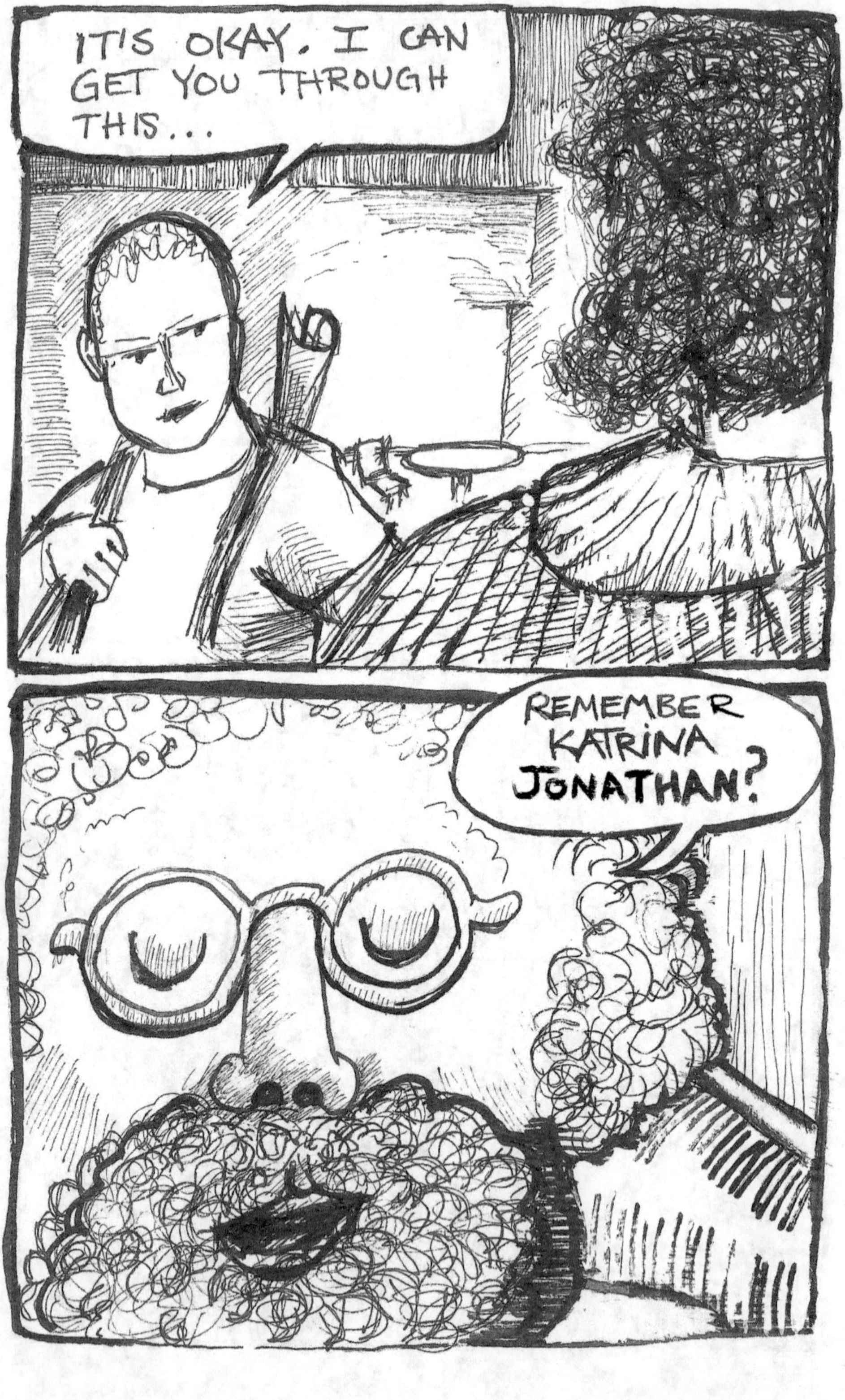
IT'S OKAY. I CAN GET YOU THROUGH THIS...
REMEMBER KATRINA JONATHAN?

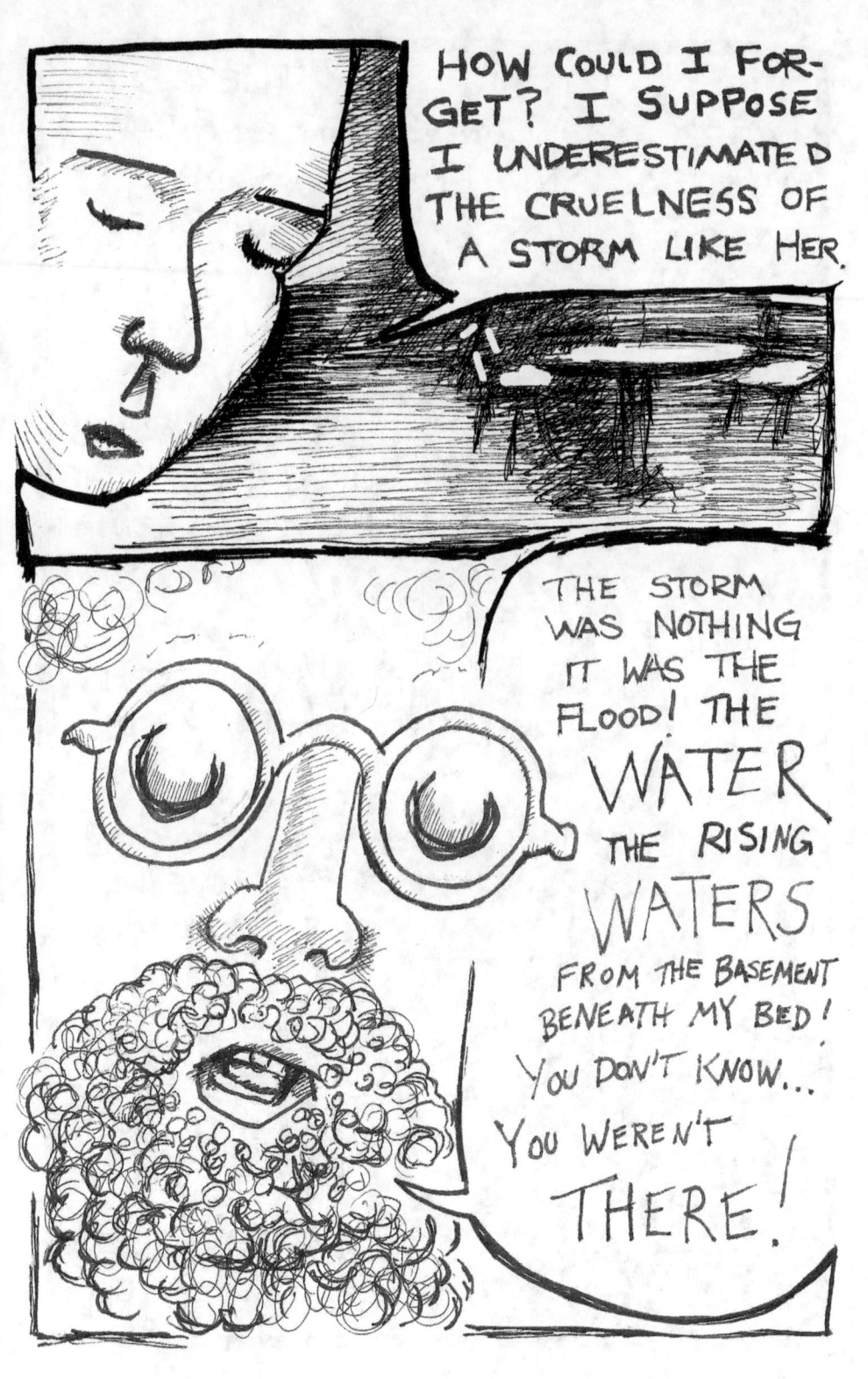

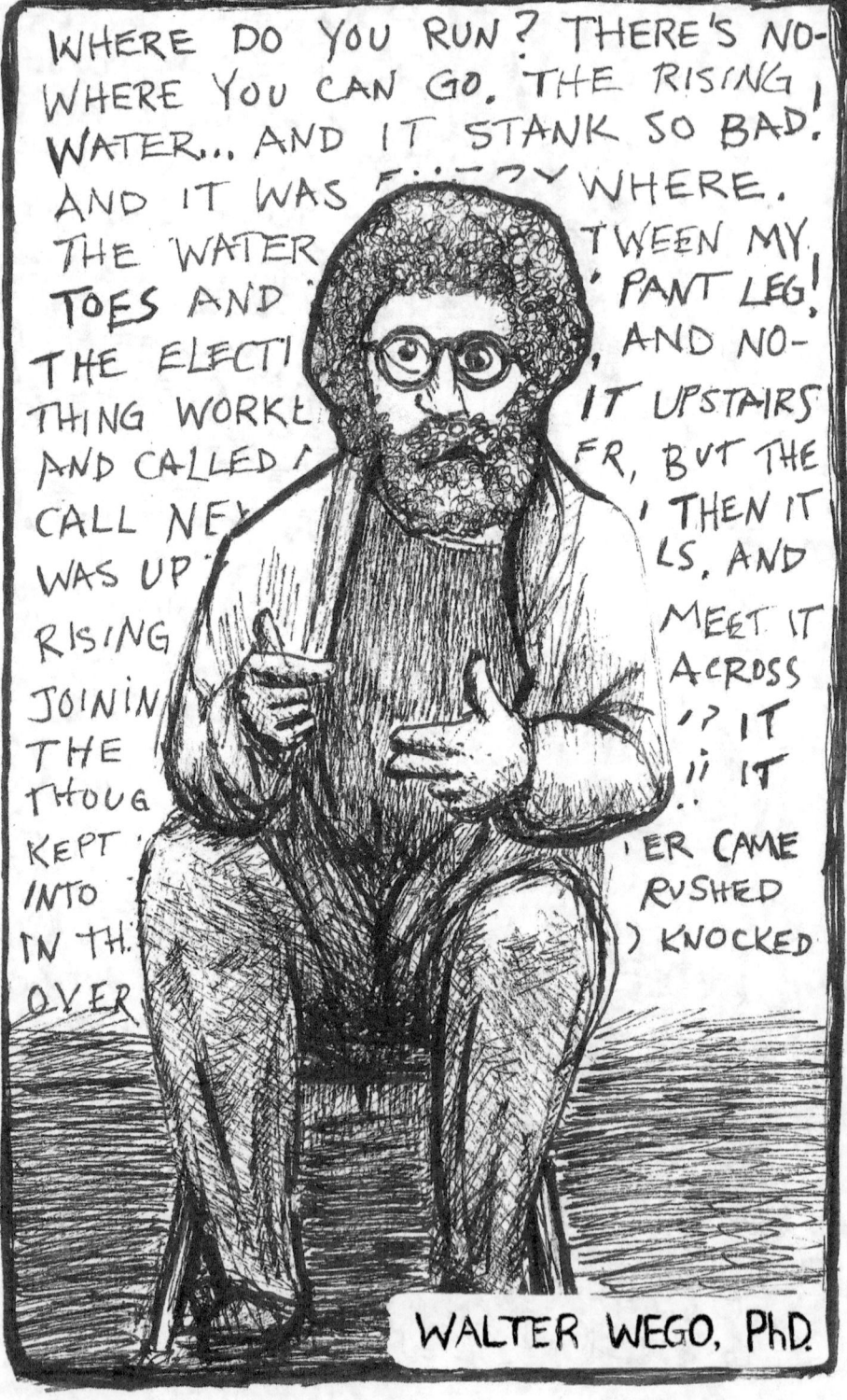

WALTER WEGO, PhD.

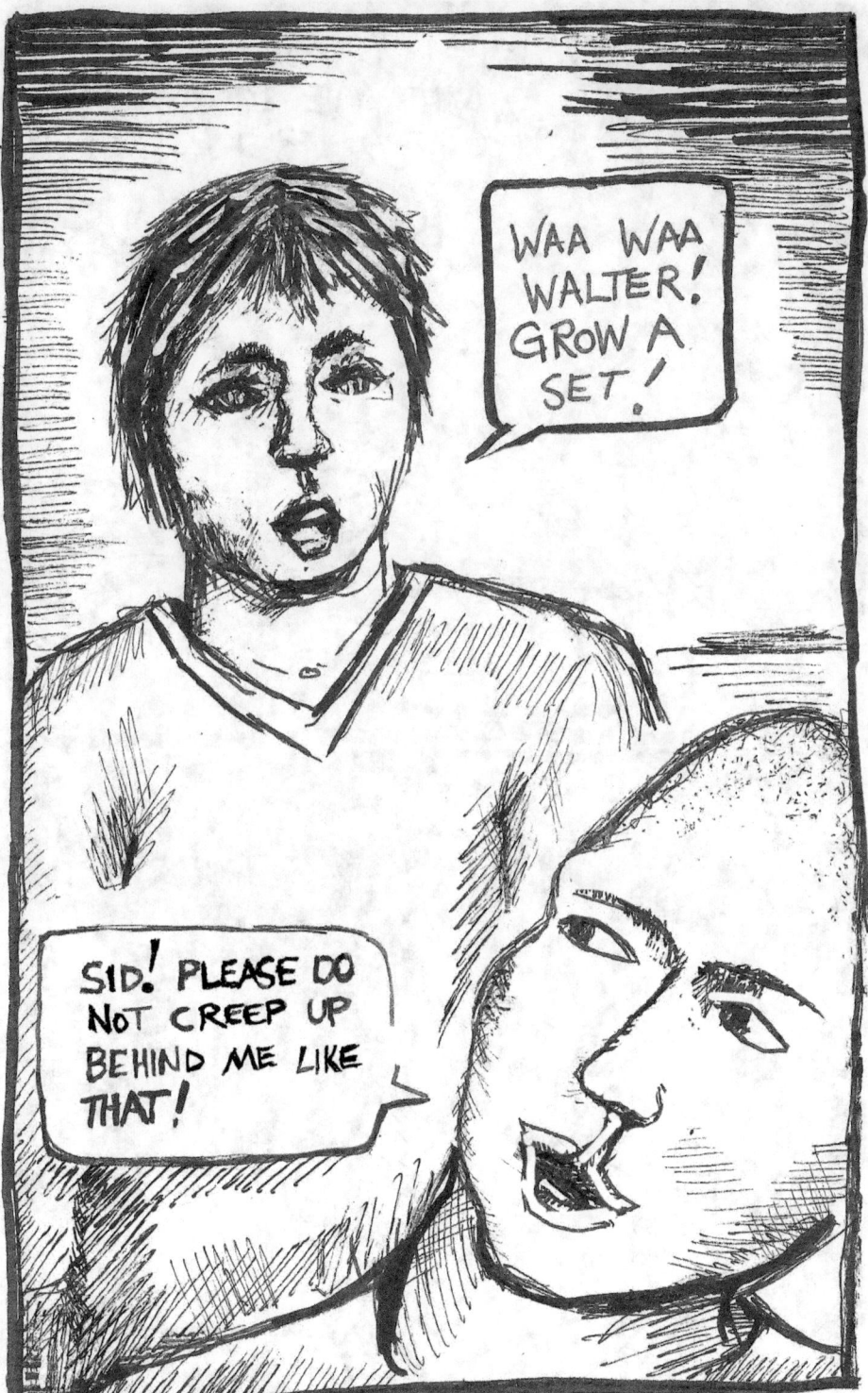

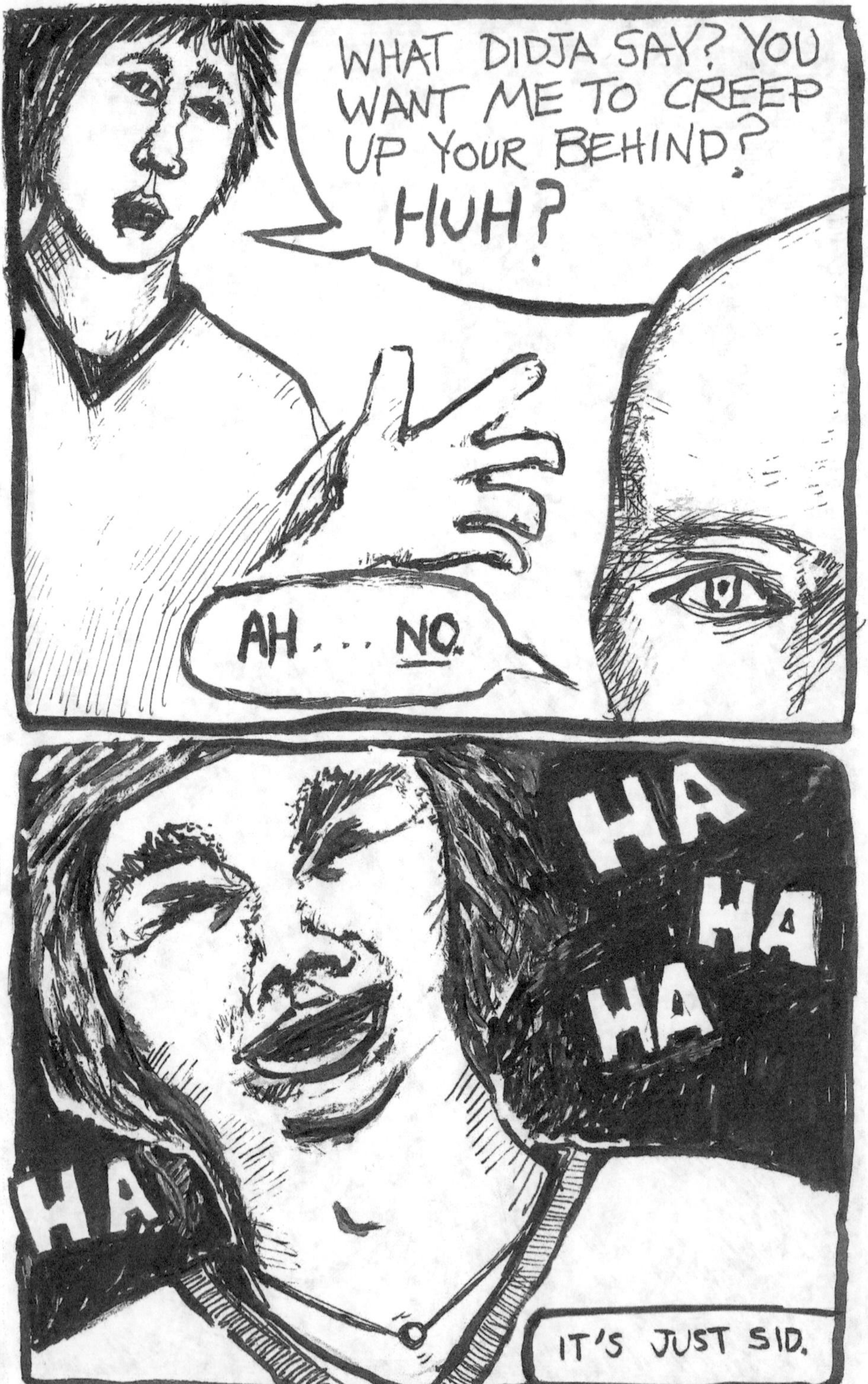
WHAT DIDJA SAY? YOU WANT ME TO CREEP UP YOUR BEHIND? HUH?
AH... NO.
HA HA HA
HA
IT'S JUST SID.

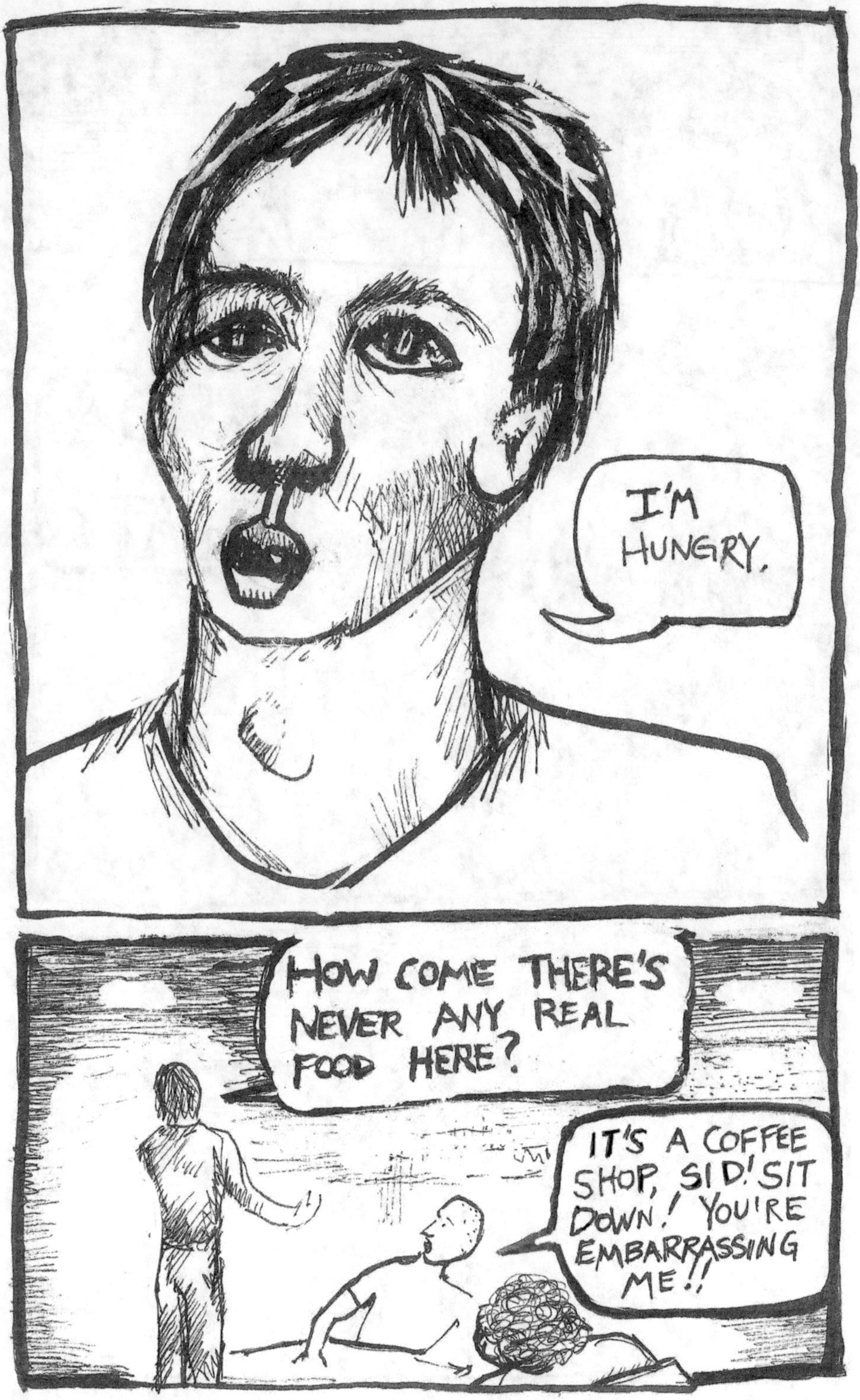

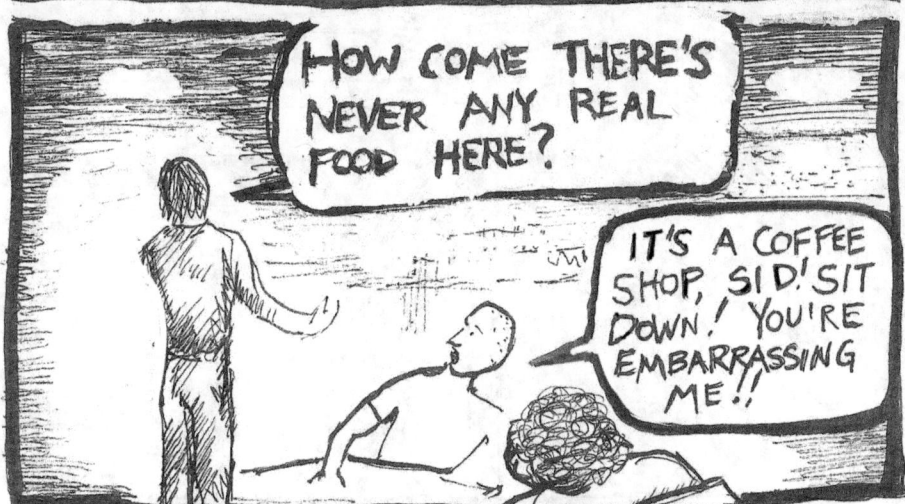

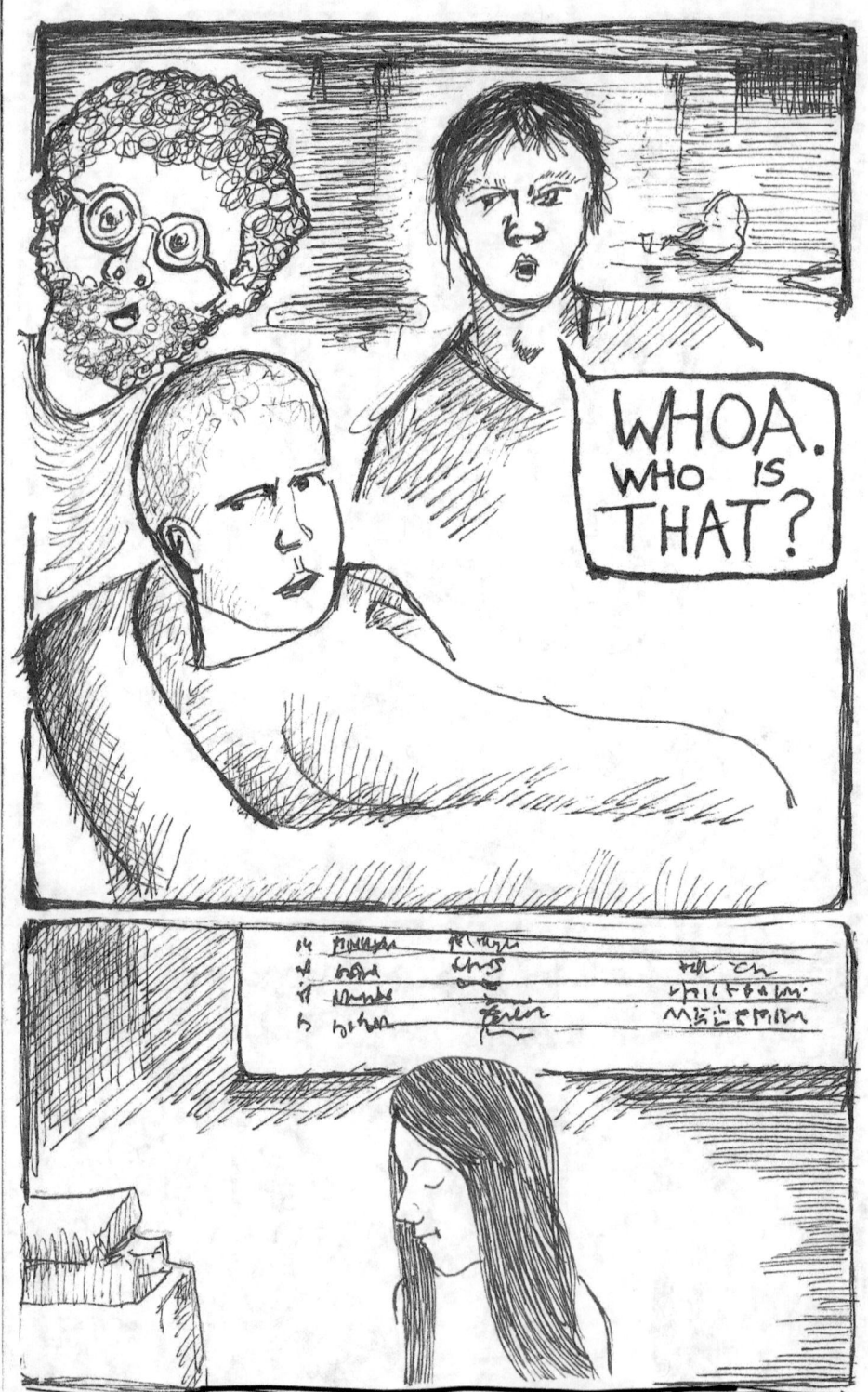

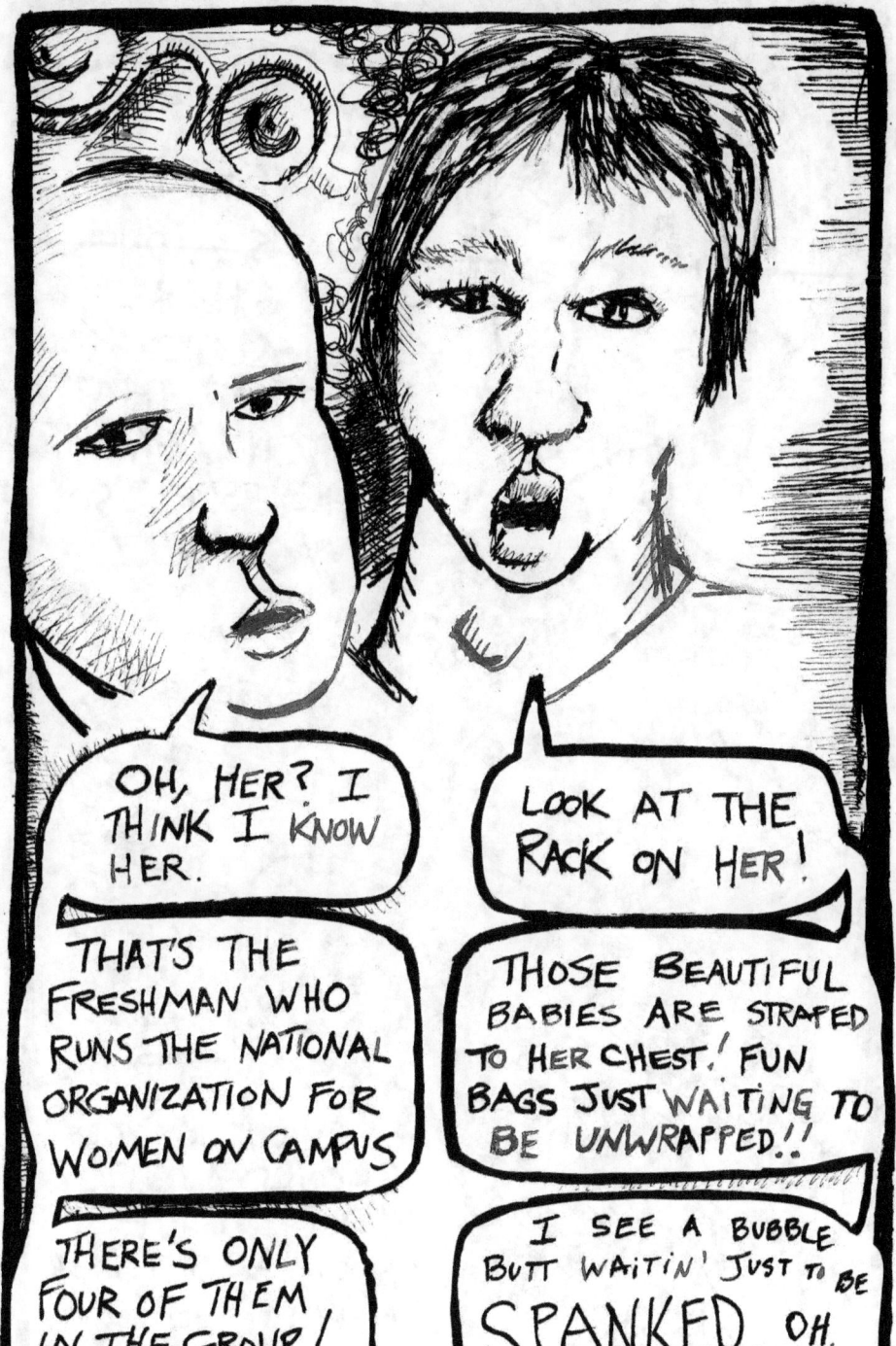

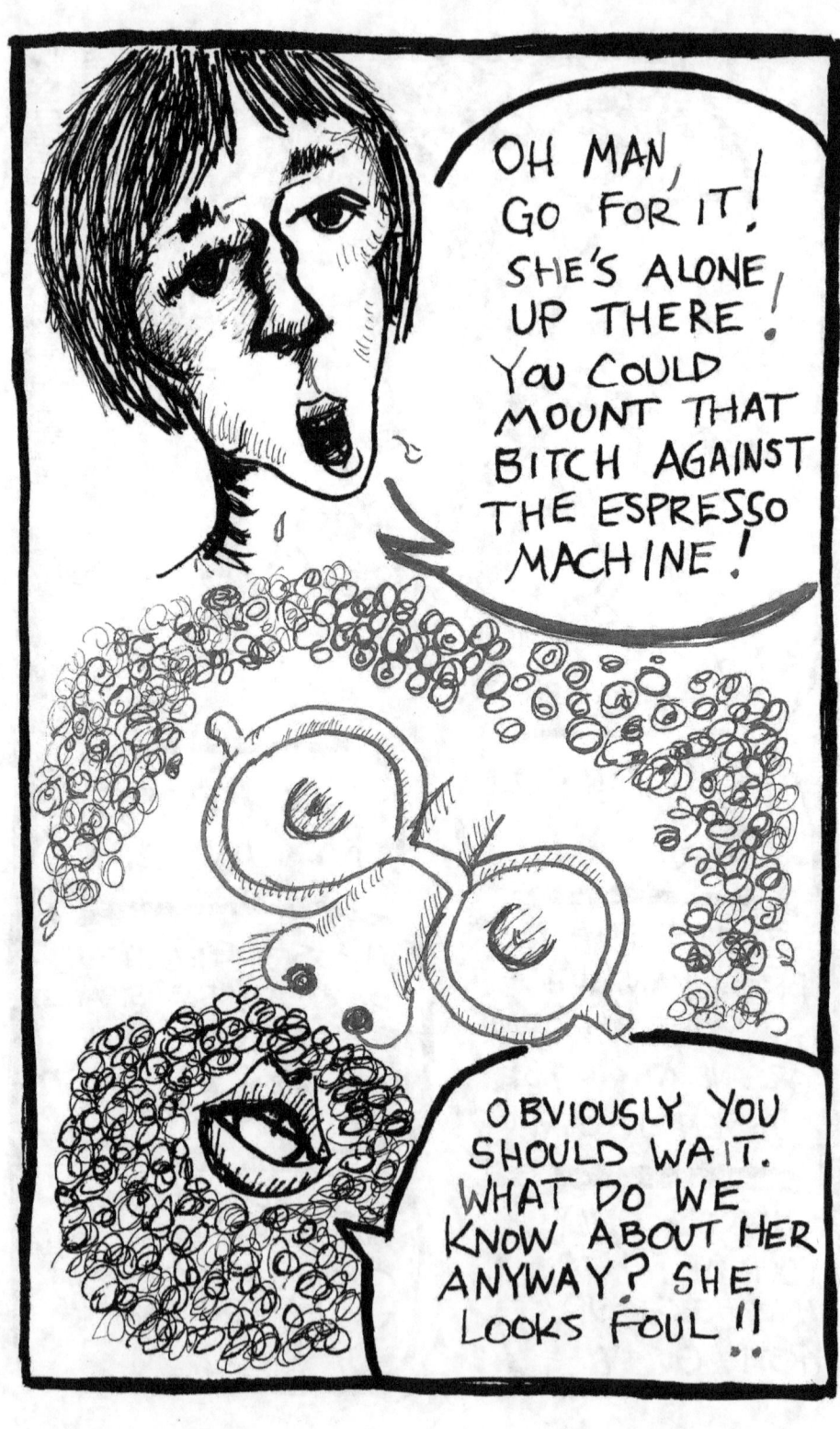

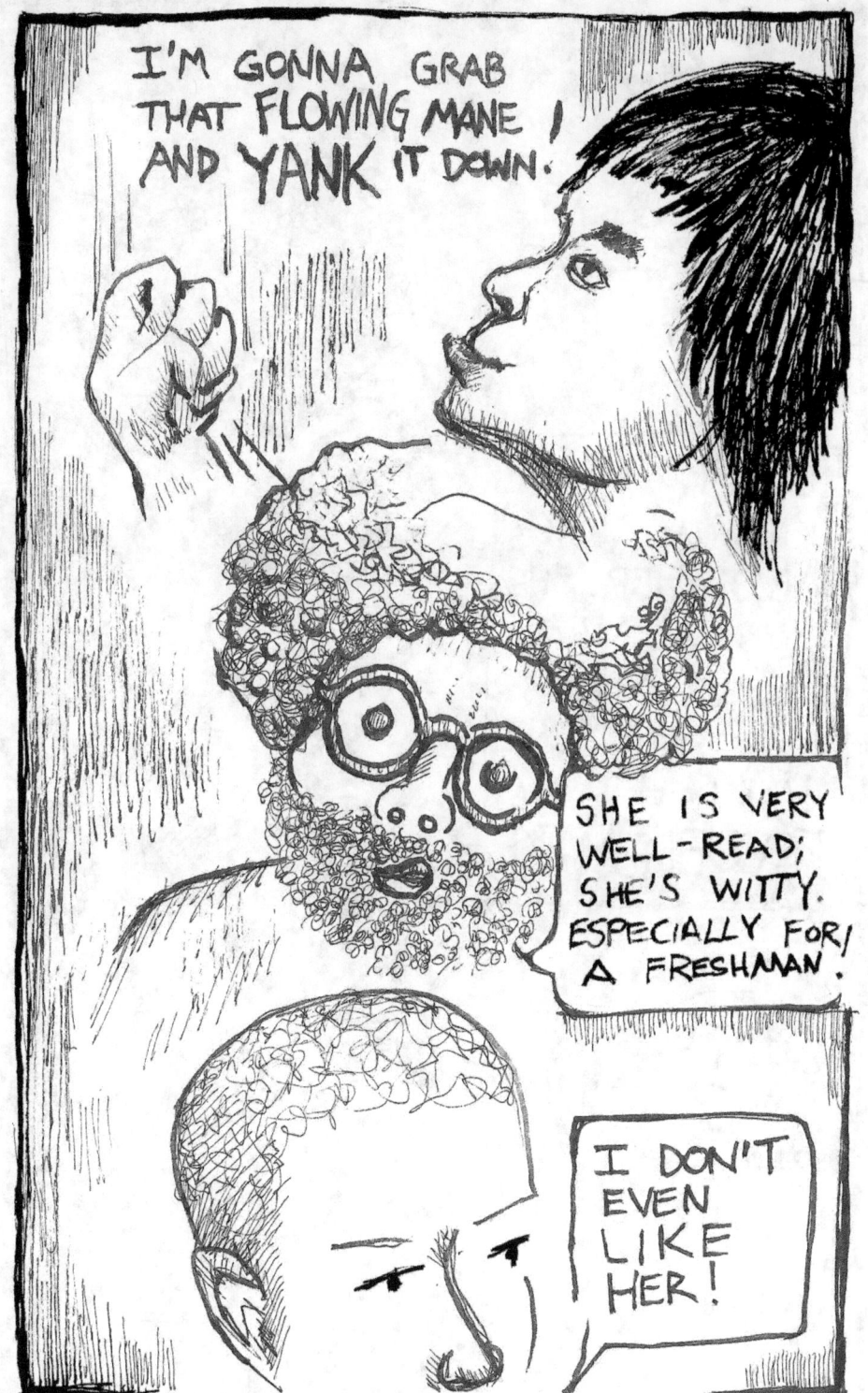

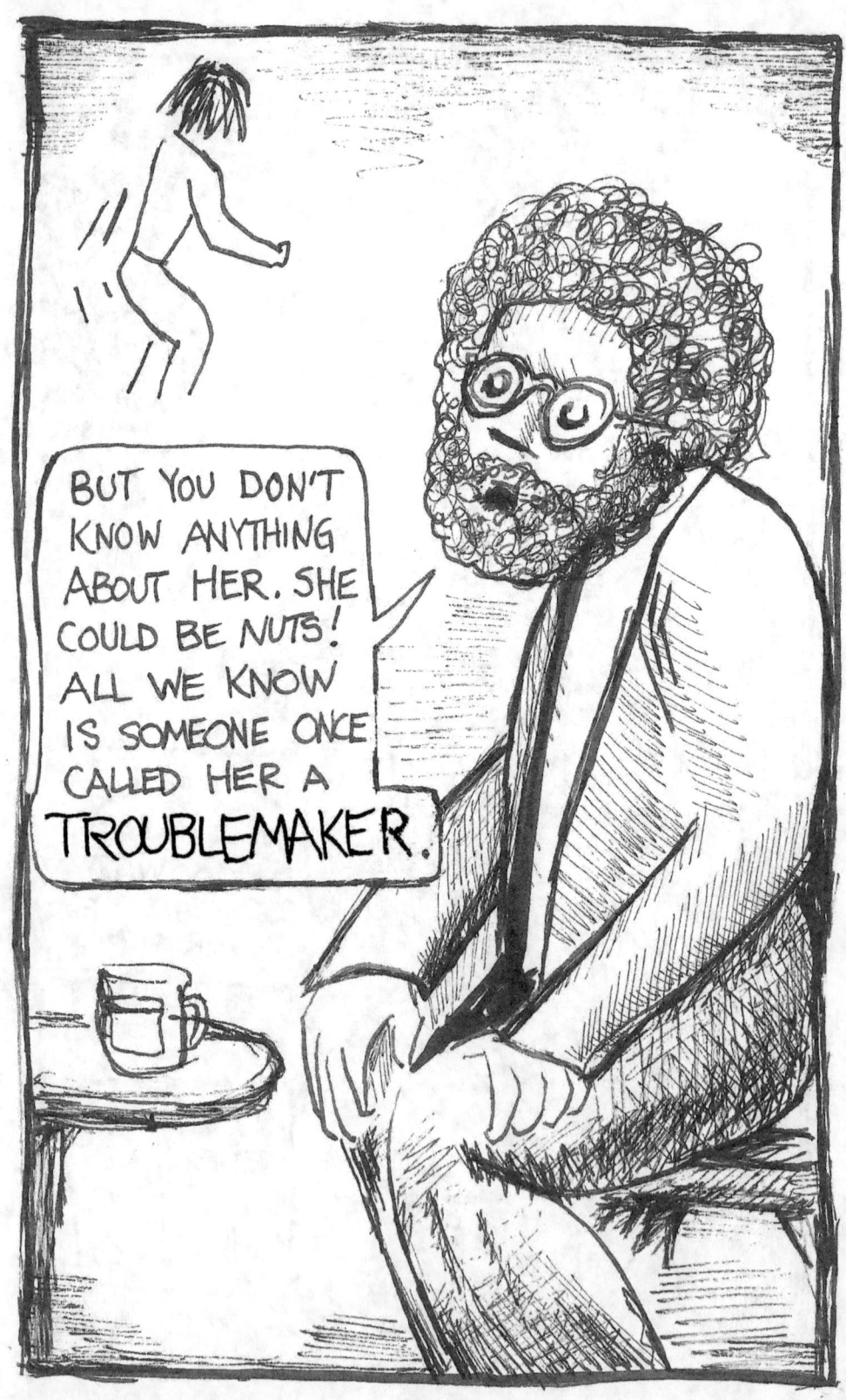

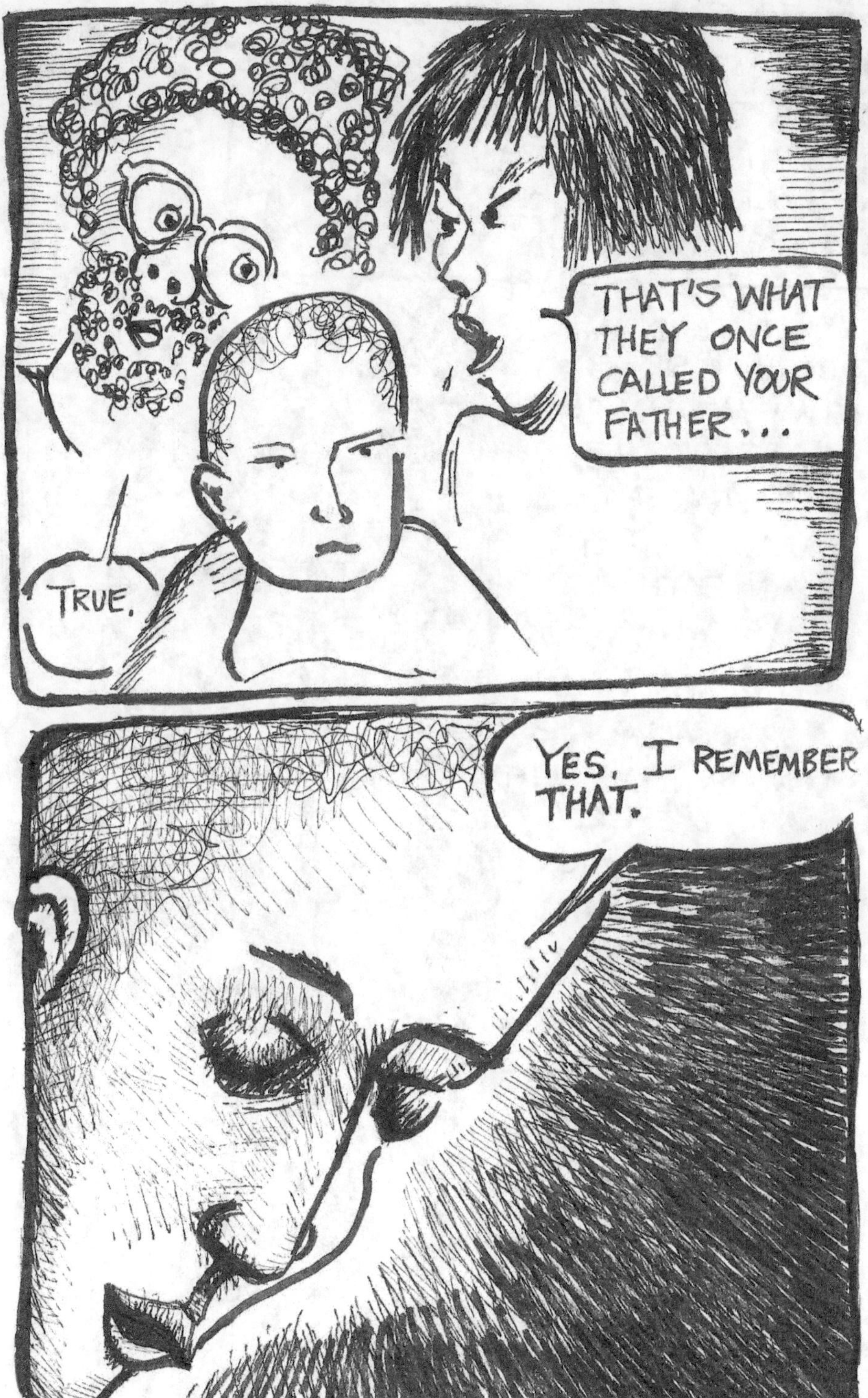
THAT'S WHAT THEY ONCE CALLED YOUR FATHER...
TRUE.
YES, I REMEMBER THAT.

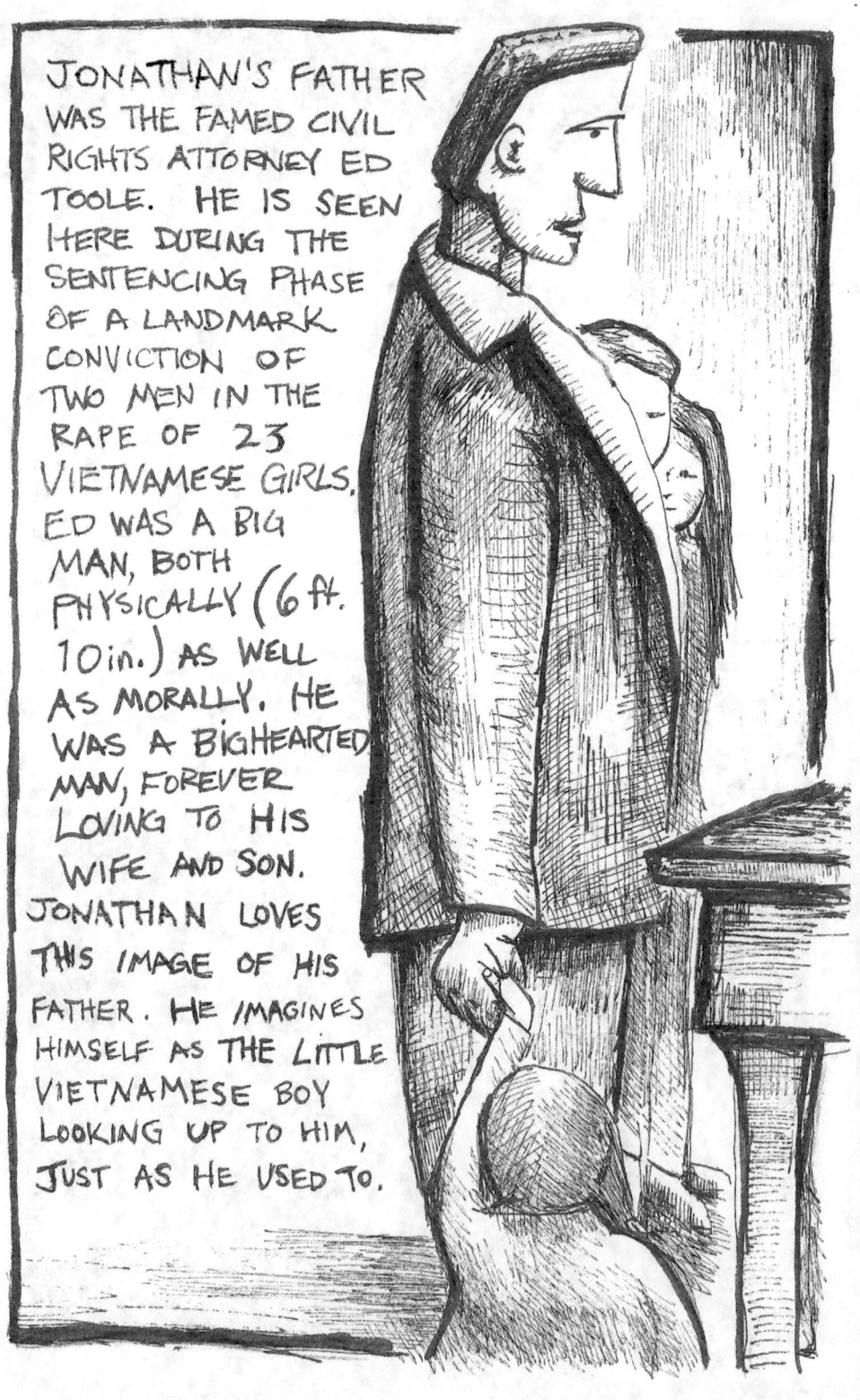

JONATHAN'S FATHER WAS THE FAMED CIVIL RIGHTS ATTORNEY ED TOOLE. HE IS SEEN HERE DURING THE SENTENCING PHASE OF A LANDMARK CONVICTION OF TWO MEN IN THE RAPE OF 23 VIETNAMESE GIRLS. ED WAS A BIG MAN, BOTH PHYSICALLY (6 ft. 10 in.) AS WELL AS MORALLY. HE WAS A BIGHEARTED MAN, FOREVER LOVING TO HIS WIFE AND SON. JONATHAN LOVES THIS IMAGE OF HIS FATHER. HE IMAGINES HIMSELF AS THE LITTLE VIETNAMESE BOY LOOKING UP TO HIM, JUST AS HE USED TO.

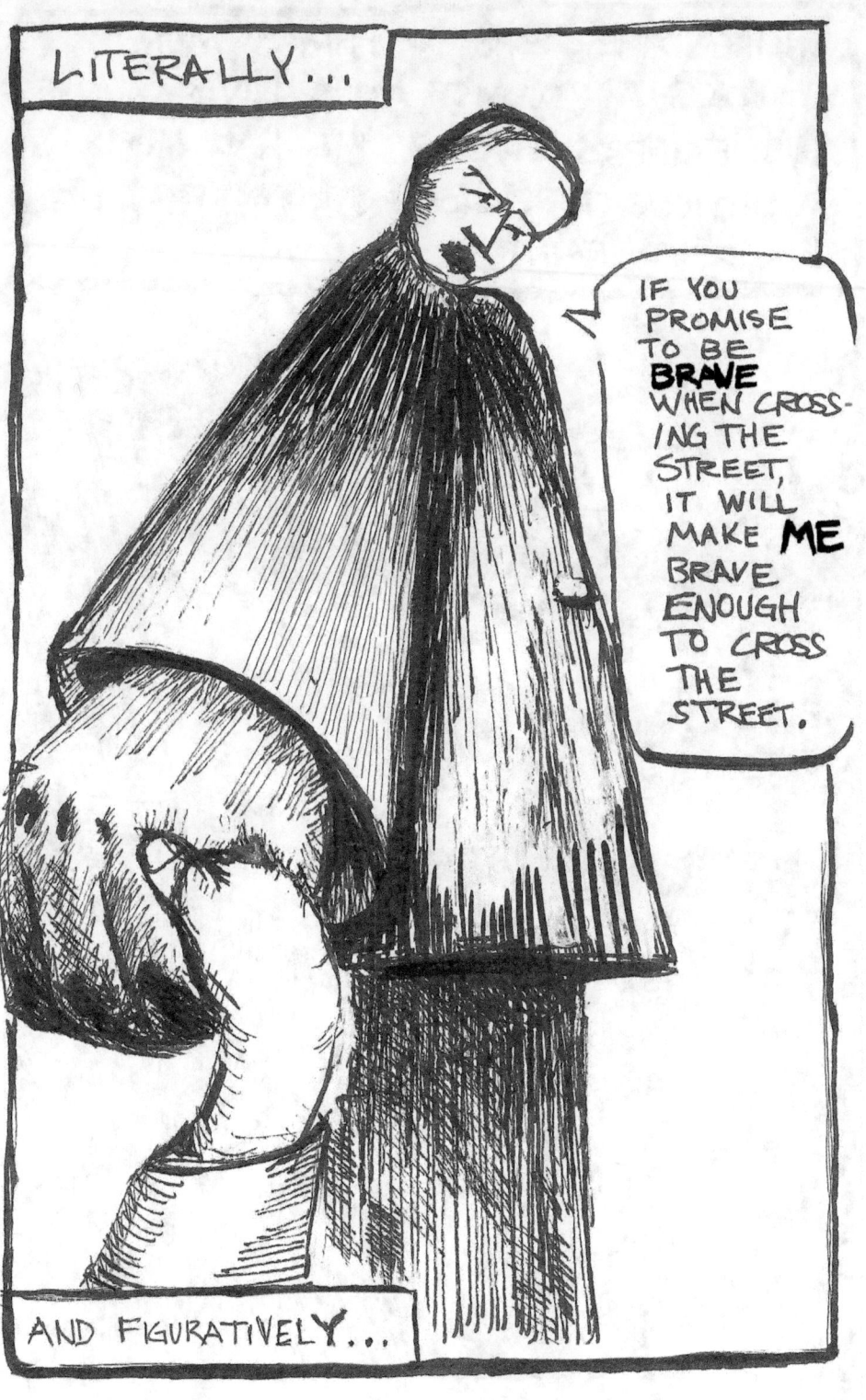

UNLIKE OTHER SONS OF FAMOUS MEN, JONATHAN DIDN'T MIND LIVING IN HIS FATHER'S SHADOW. HE HAD NO AMBITIONS TO BECOME A LAWYER. HE LIKED TO PAINT.

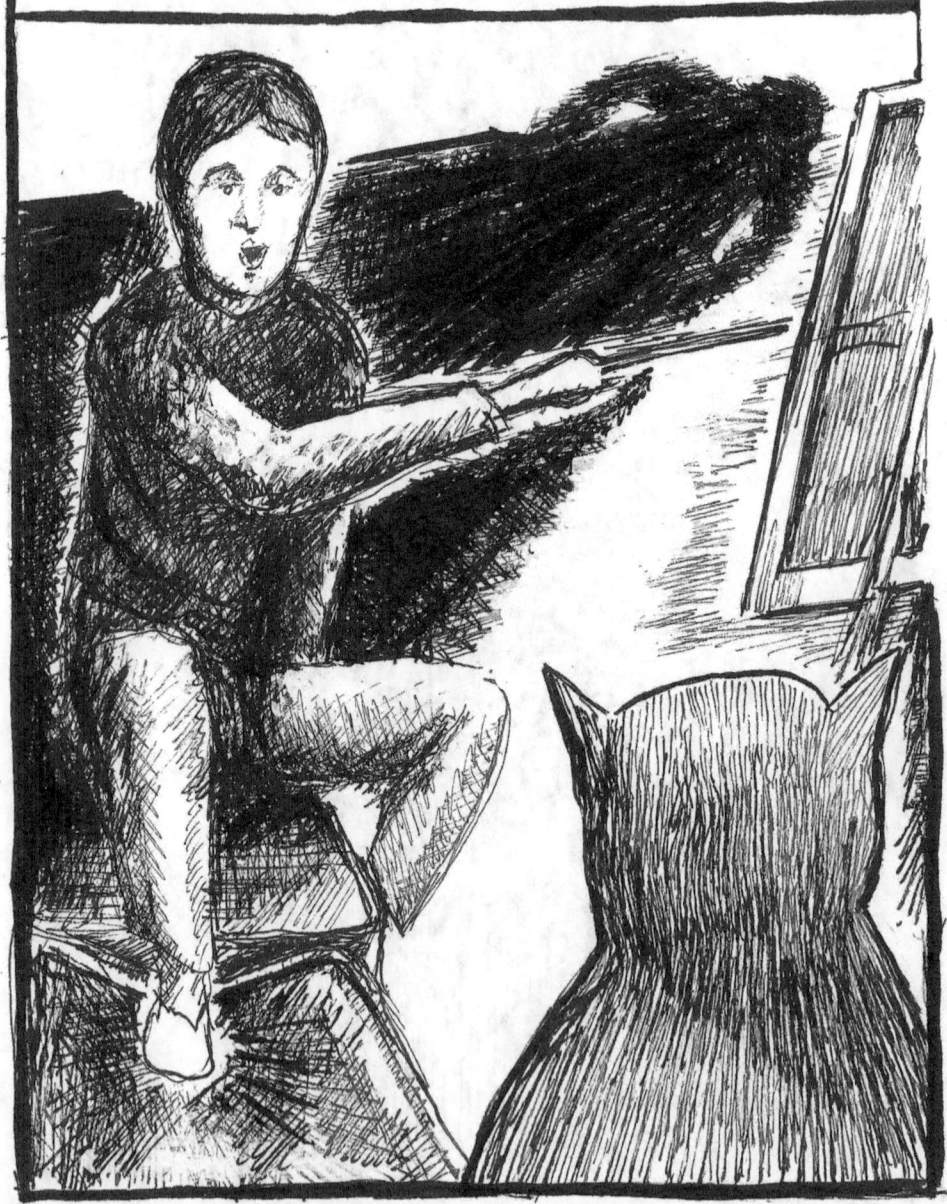

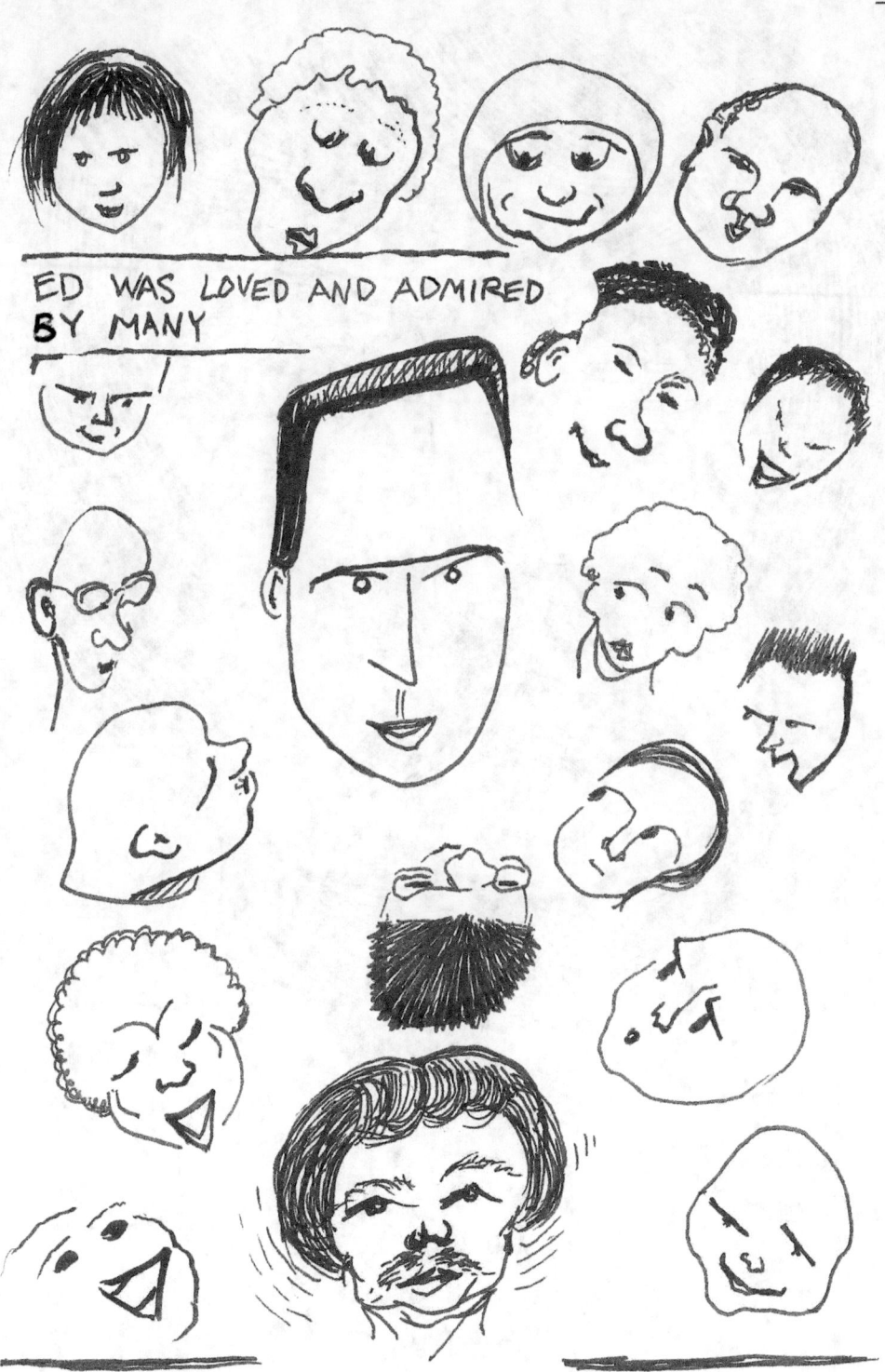

ED WAS LOVED AND ADMIRED BY MANY

BUT, THERE'S ALWAYS ONE EXCEPTION...

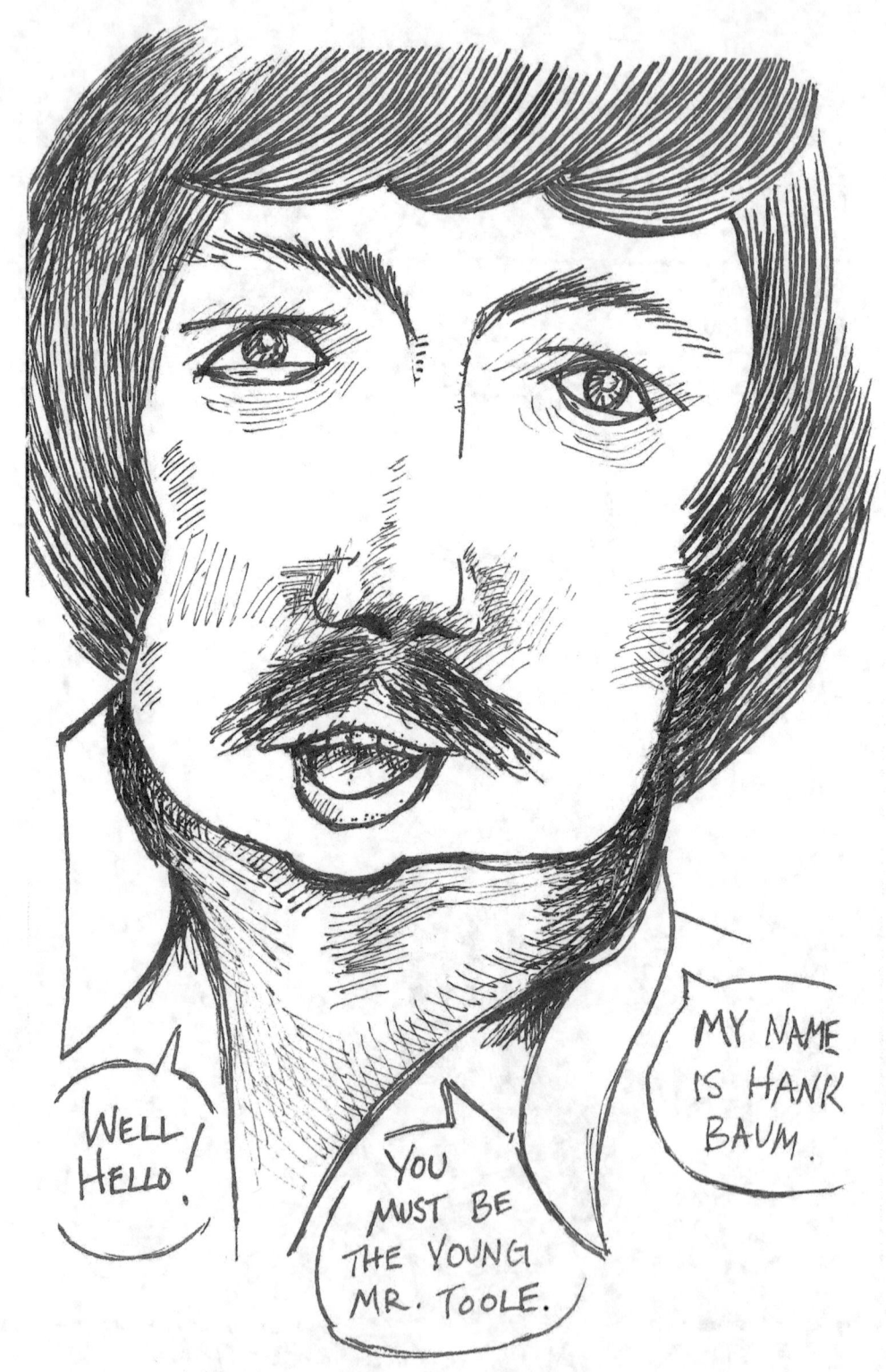

BY THE TIME I WAS 22, I HAD MY JURIS DOCTORATE AND WAS WORKING IN THE D.A.'S OFFICE. HOW ARE YOUR GRADES, YOUNG TOOLE? YOU MUST FOLLOW IN YOUR FATHER'S FOOTSTEPS. ALTHOUGH A TROUBLEMAKER, HE'S A DAMN FINE LAWYER!

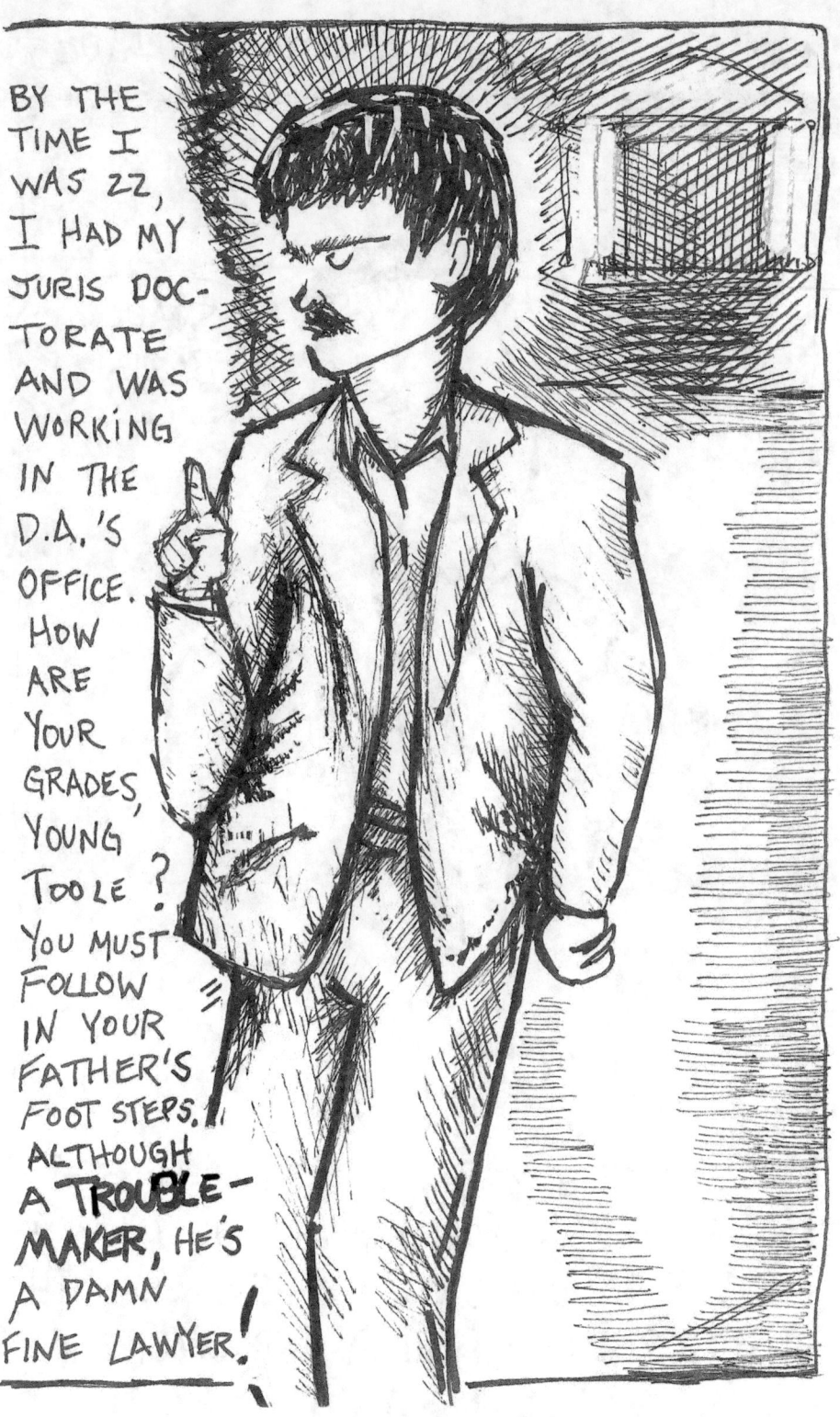

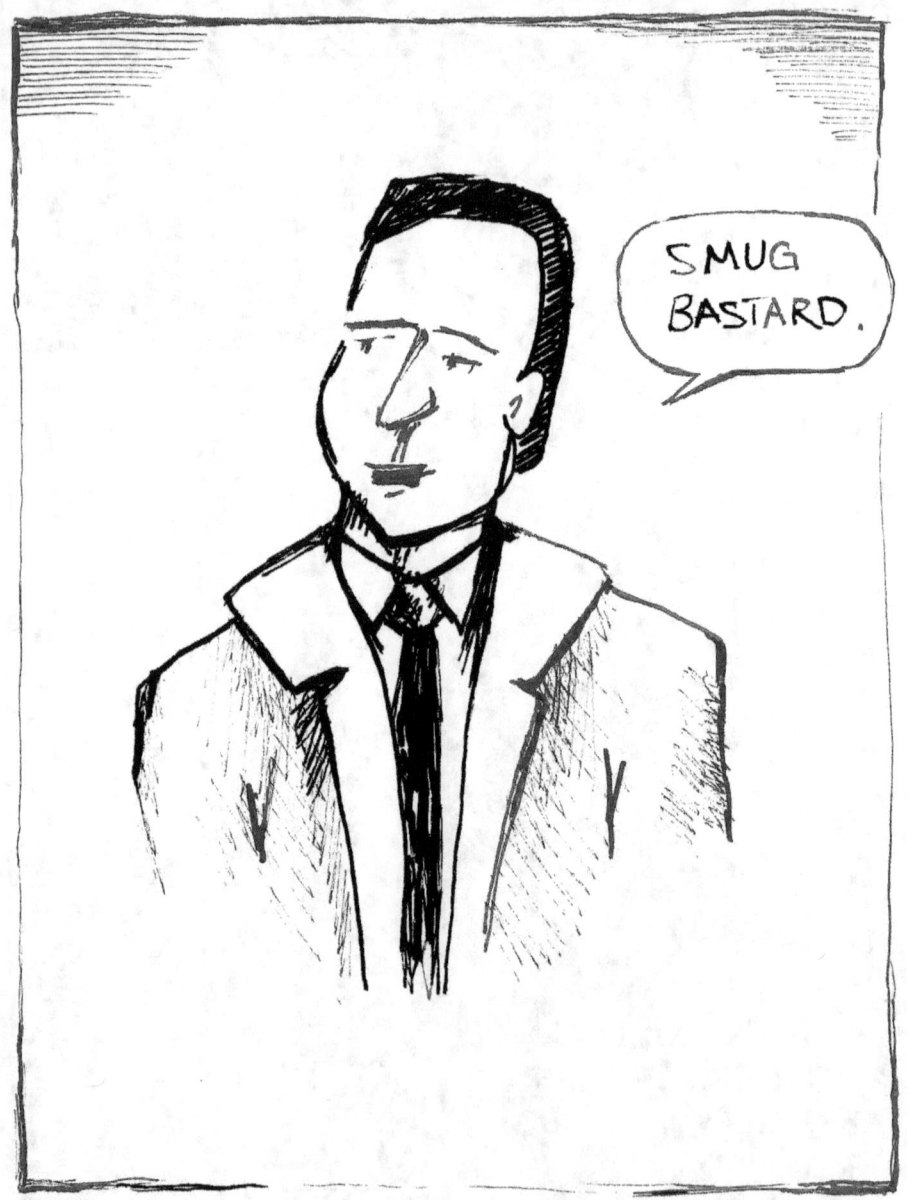

HANK WAS A FORMIDABLE FOE IN MANY OF ED'S FAMOUS CIVIL RIGHTS CASES. HE USED CRAFTY STRATEGY AND BRAGGED A LOT.

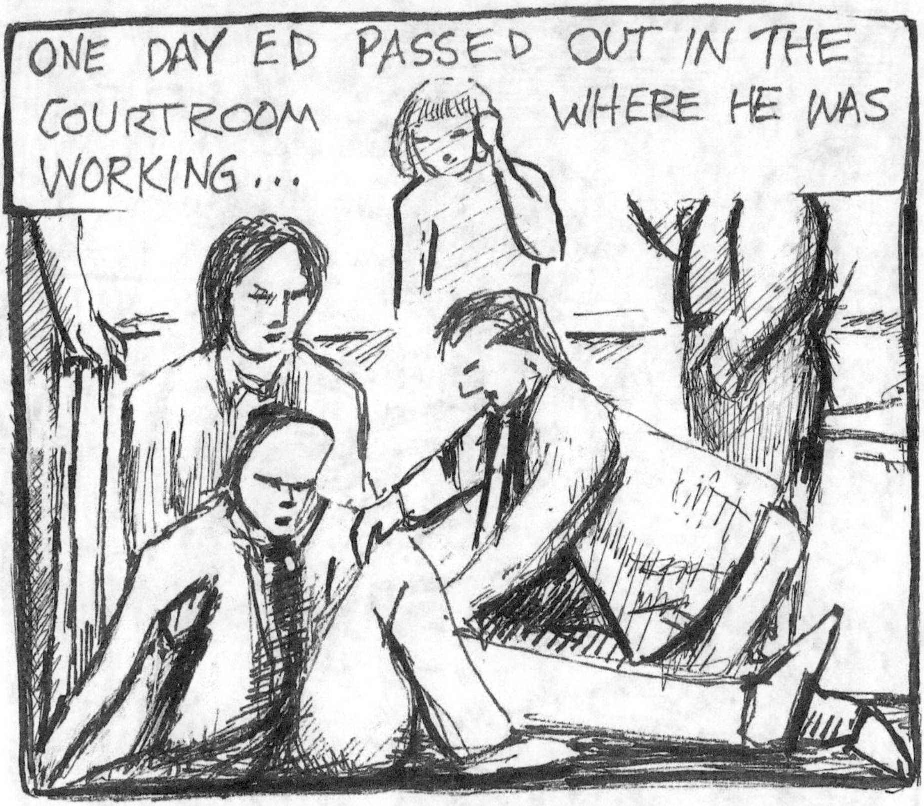

ONE DAY ED PASSED OUT IN THE COURTROOM WHERE HE WAS WORKING...

HE WAS OVERWORKED. DONE IN BY HANK'S MASTERY OF LAWYER TRICKS.

A BIT OF A SHOWBOAT, DON'T YOU THINK? COL-LASPING IN A COURT ROOM?

I MOVE FOR A MISTRIAL.

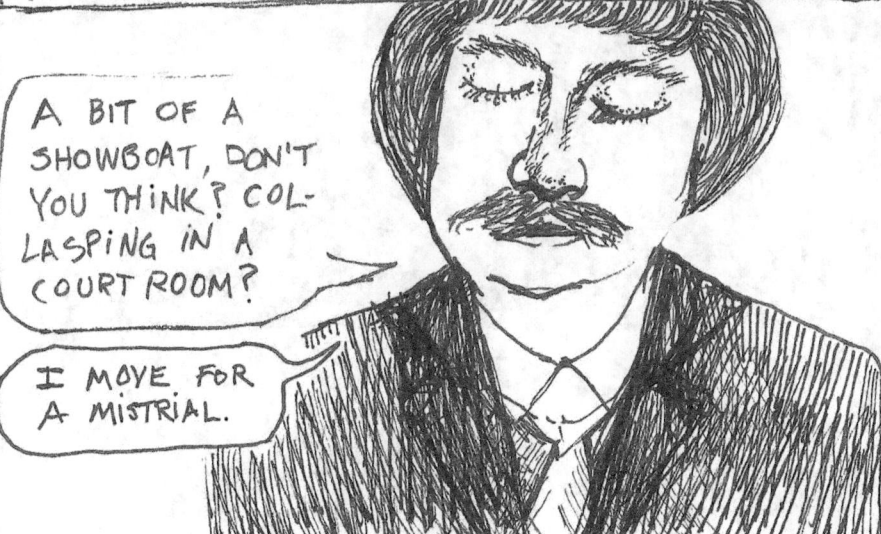

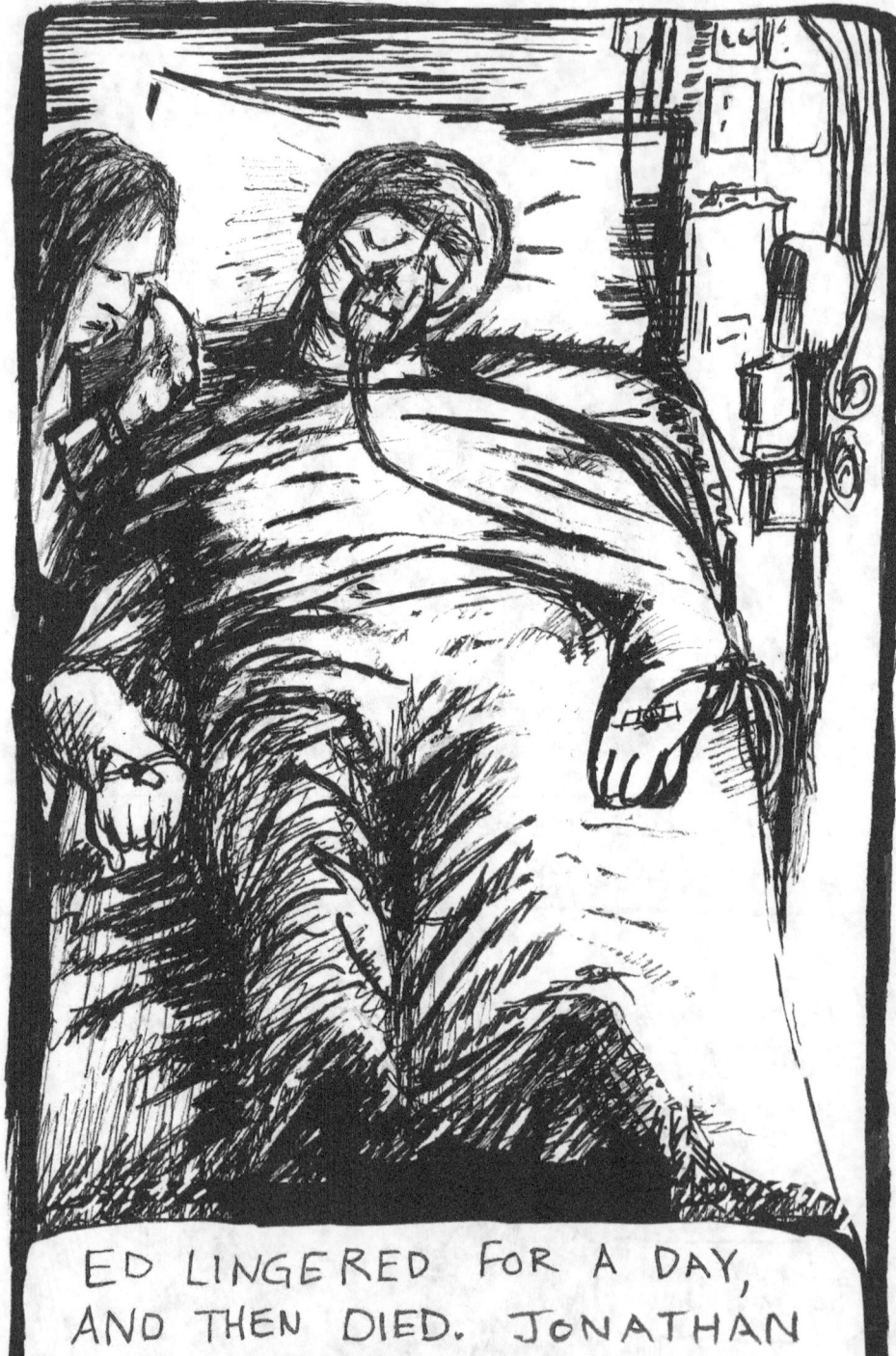

ED LINGERED FOR A DAY, AND THEN DIED. JONATHAN WOULD NEVER BE THE SAME.

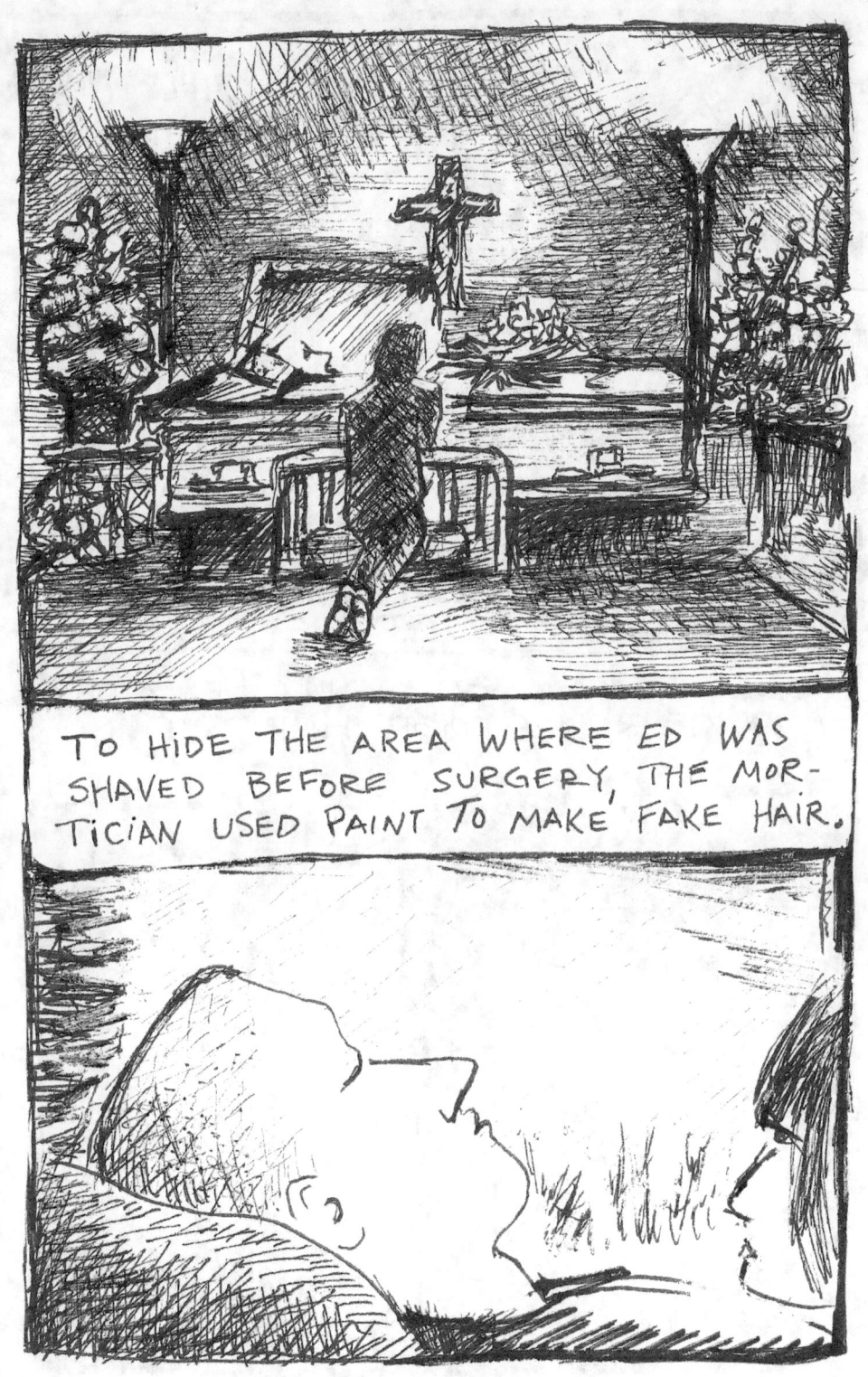

TO HIDE THE AREA WHERE ED WAS SHAVED BEFORE SURGERY, THE MORTICIAN USED PAINT TO MAKE FAKE HAIR.

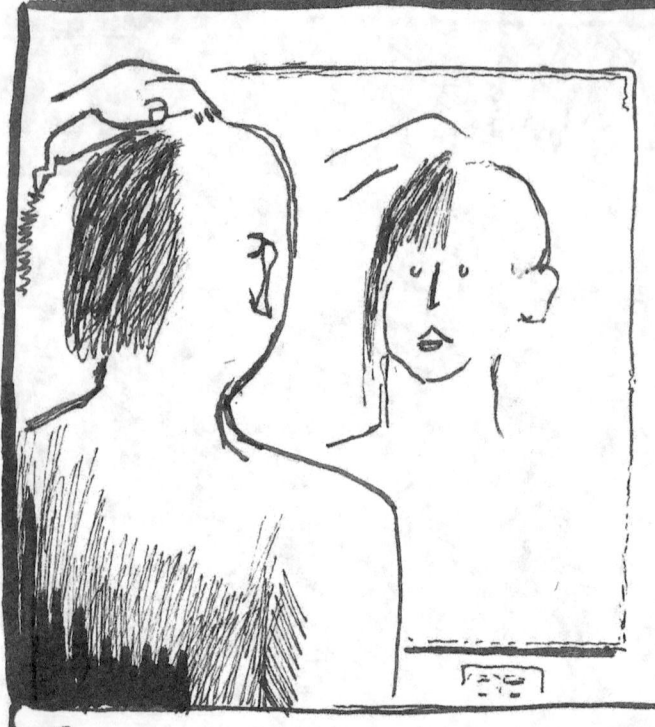

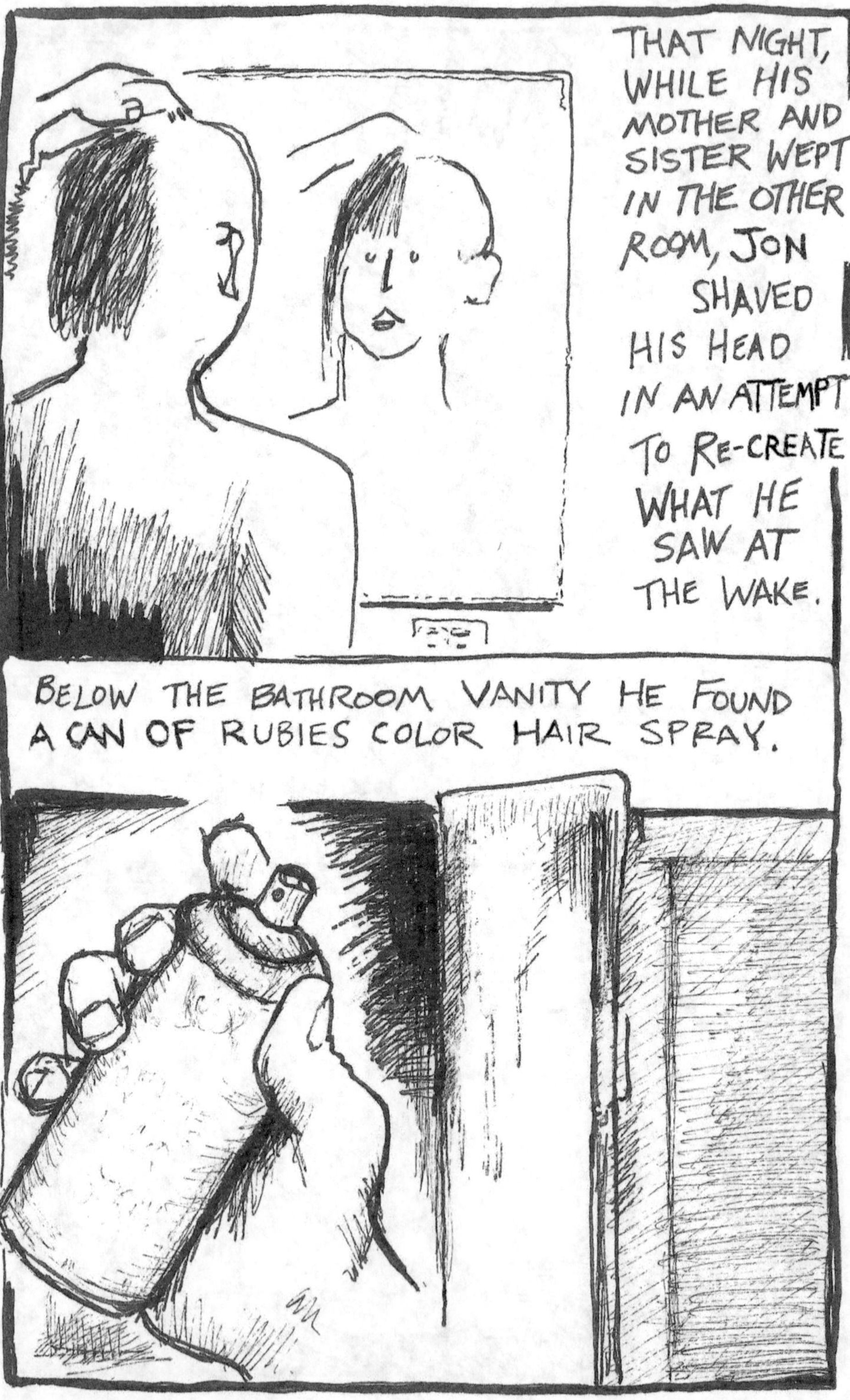

THAT NIGHT, WHILE HIS MOTHER AND SISTER WEPT IN THE OTHER ROOM, JON SHAVED HIS HEAD IN AN ATTEMPT TO RE-CREATE WHAT HE SAW AT THE WAKE.

BELOW THE BATHROOM VANITY HE FOUND A CAN OF RUBIES COLOR HAIR SPRAY.

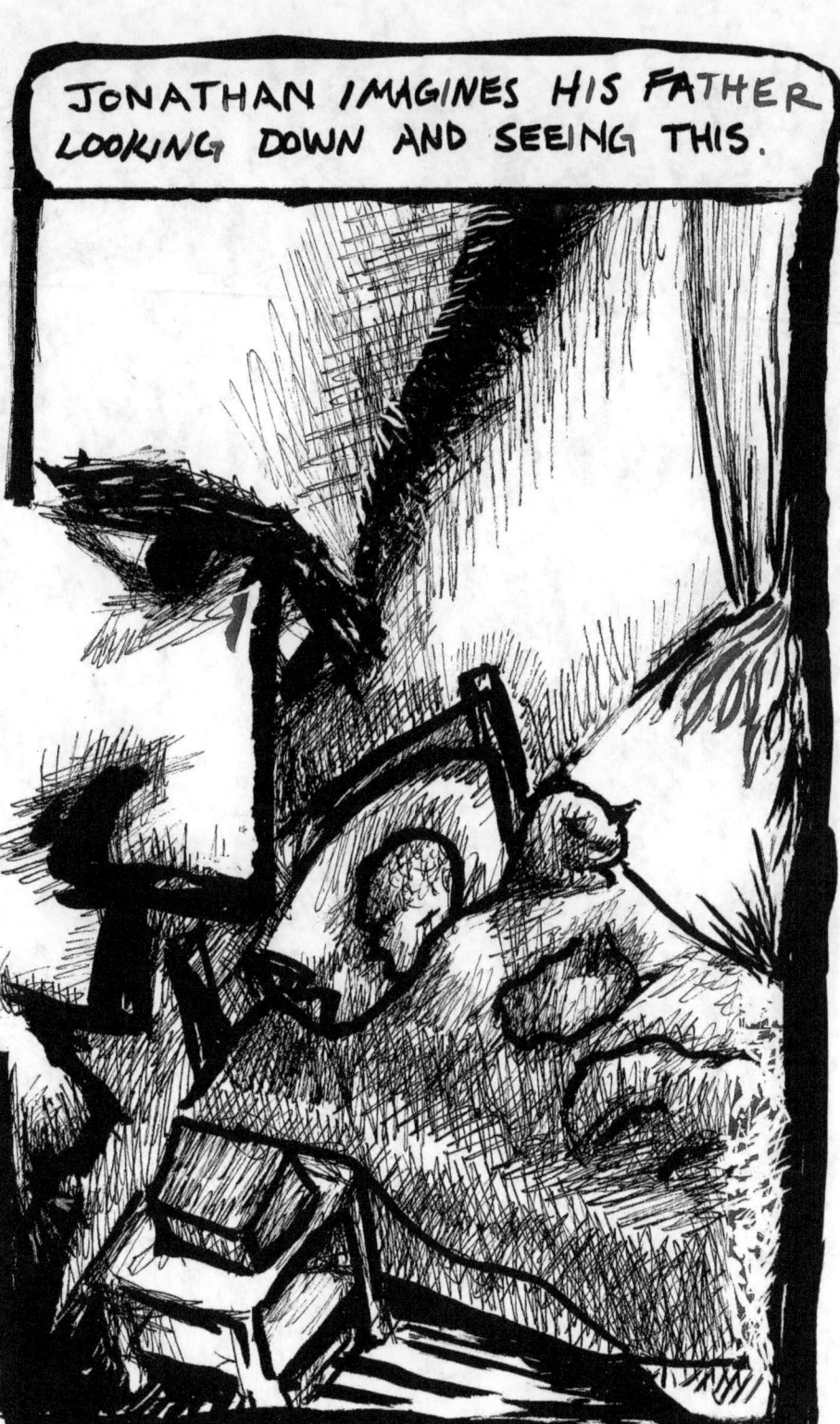

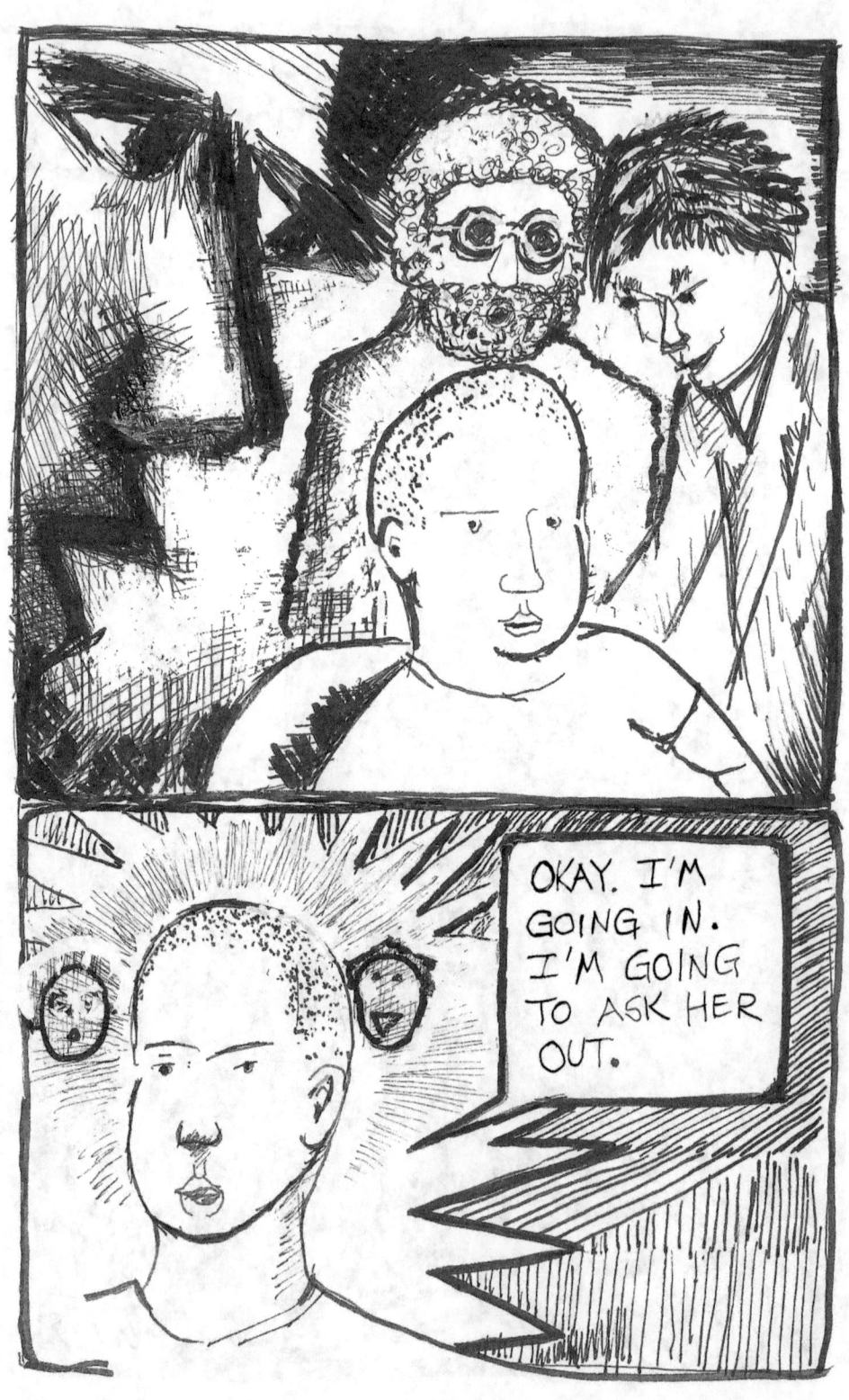

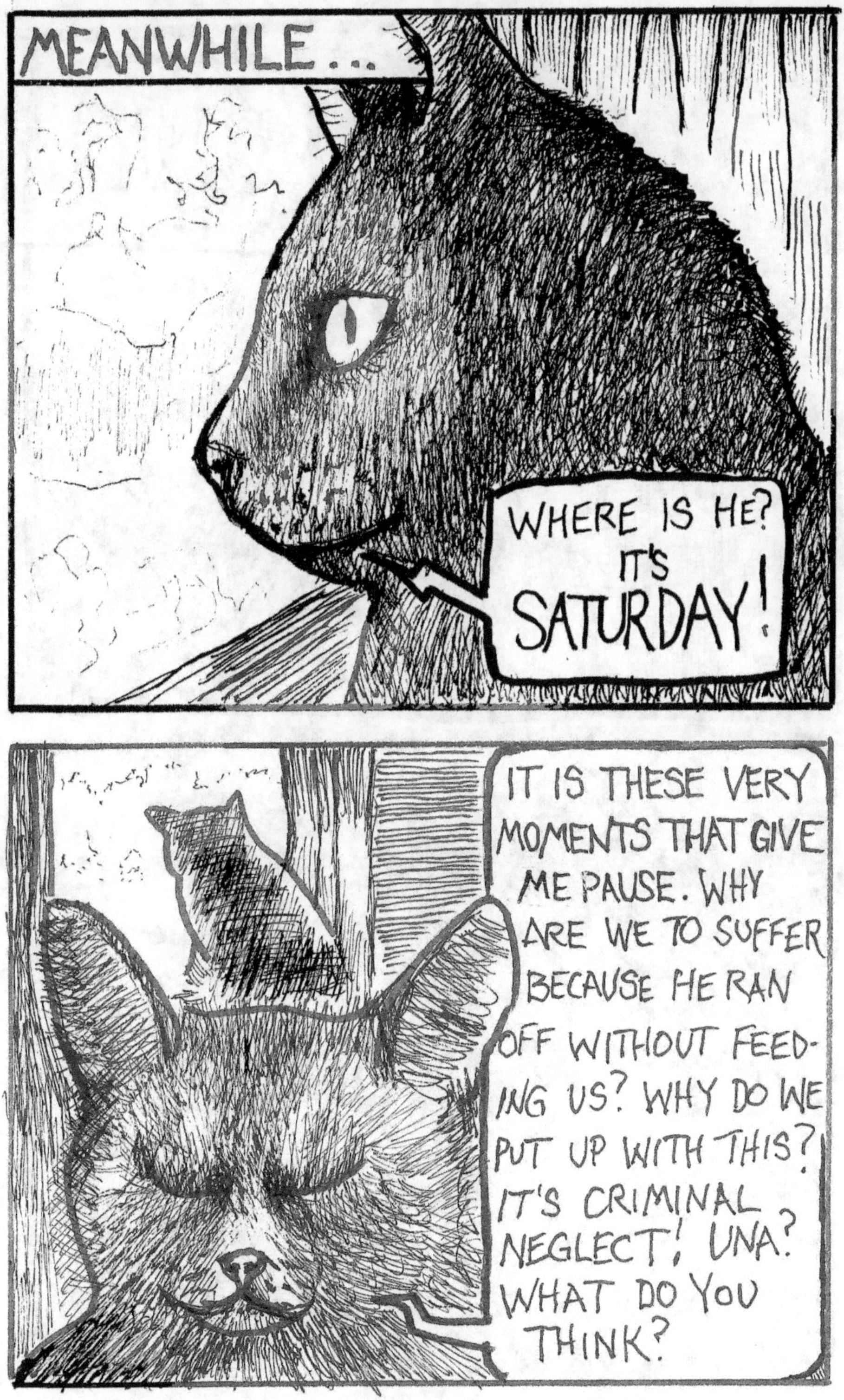

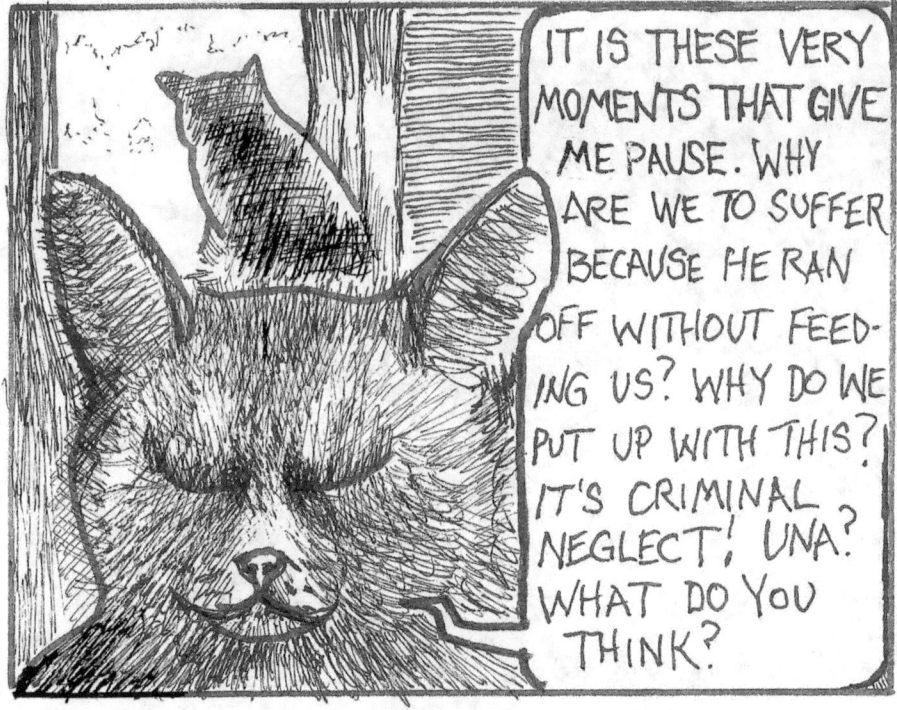

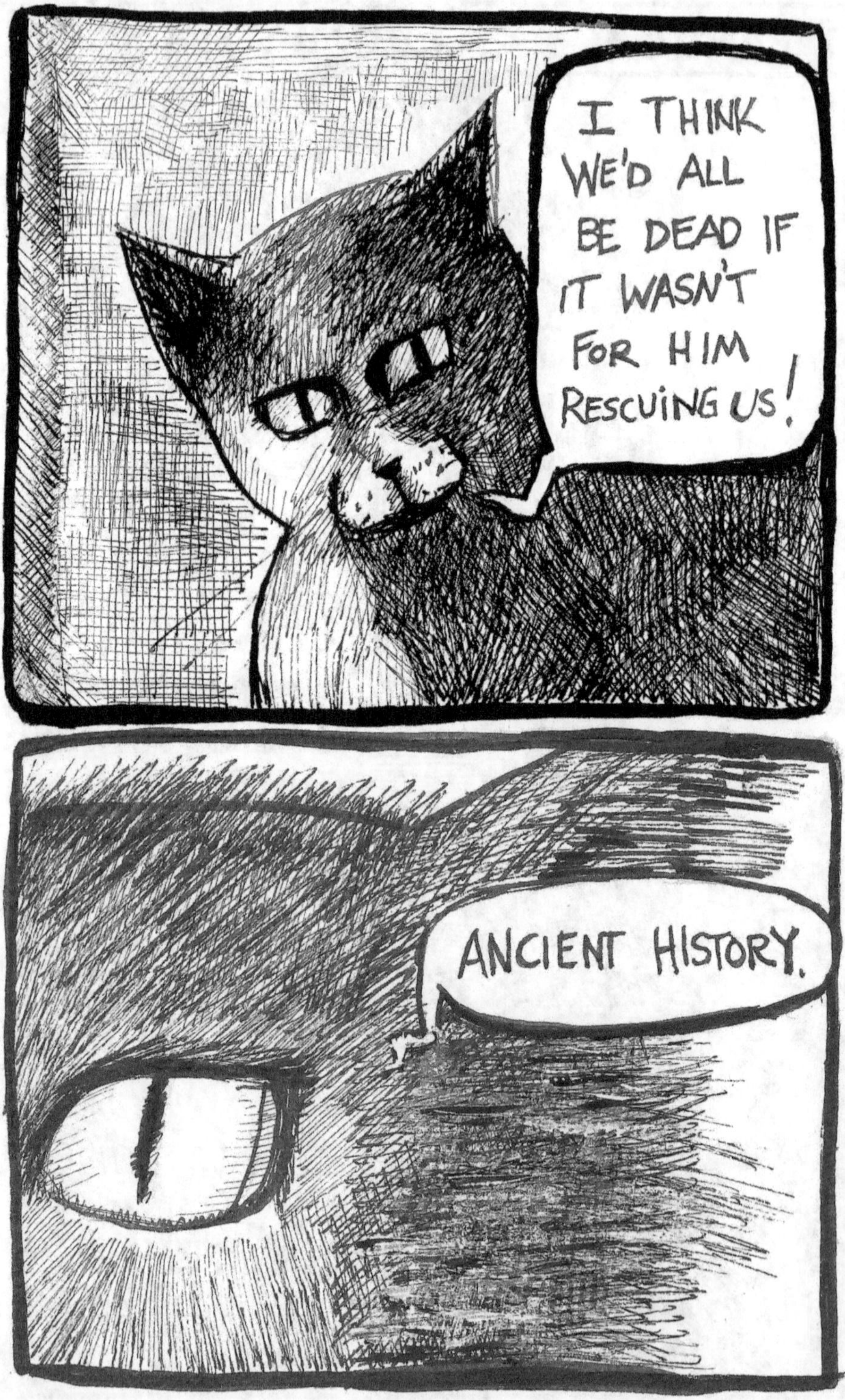

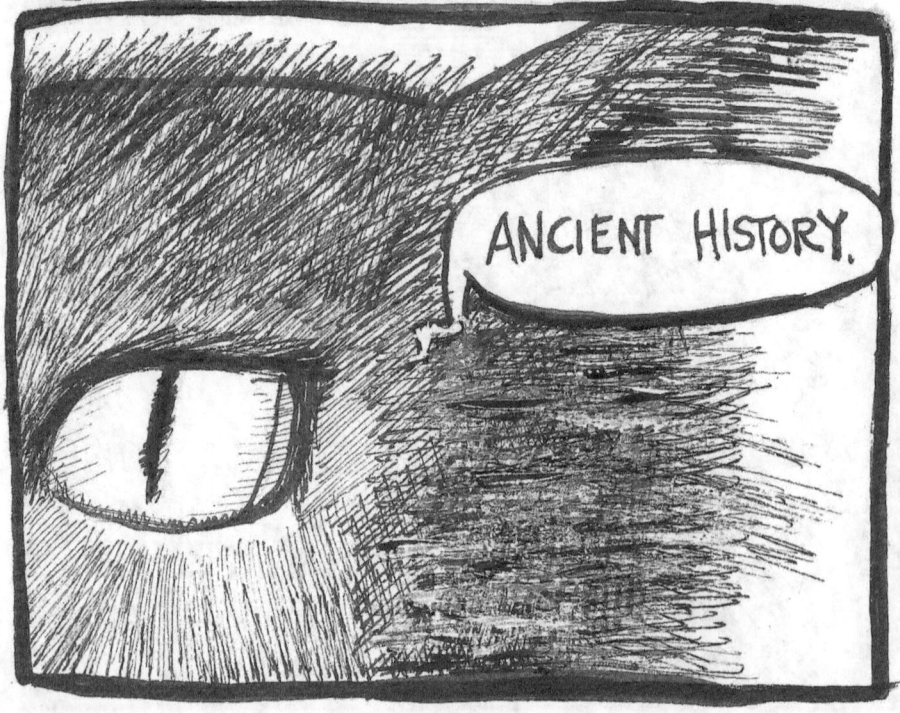

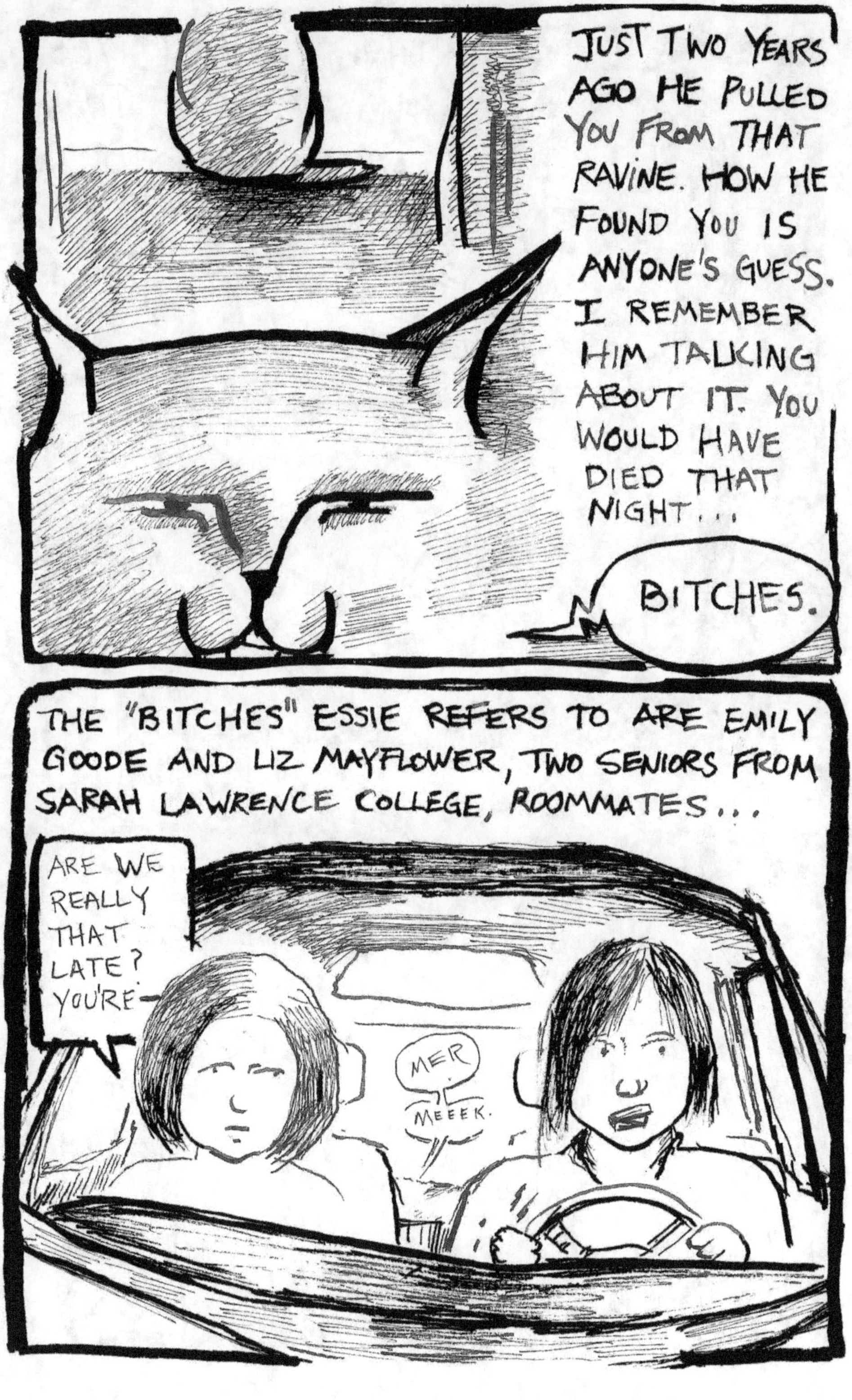

JUST TWO YEARS AGO HE PULLED YOU FROM THAT RAVINE. HOW HE FOUND YOU IS ANYONE'S GUESS. I REMEMBER HIM TALKING ABOUT IT. YOU WOULD HAVE DIED THAT NIGHT...

BITCHES.

THE "BITCHES" ESSIE REFERS TO ARE EMILY GOODE AND LIZ MAYFLOWER, TWO SENIORS FROM SARAH LAWRENCE COLLEGE, ROOMMATES...

ARE WE REALLY THAT LATE? YOU'RE—

MER MEEEK.

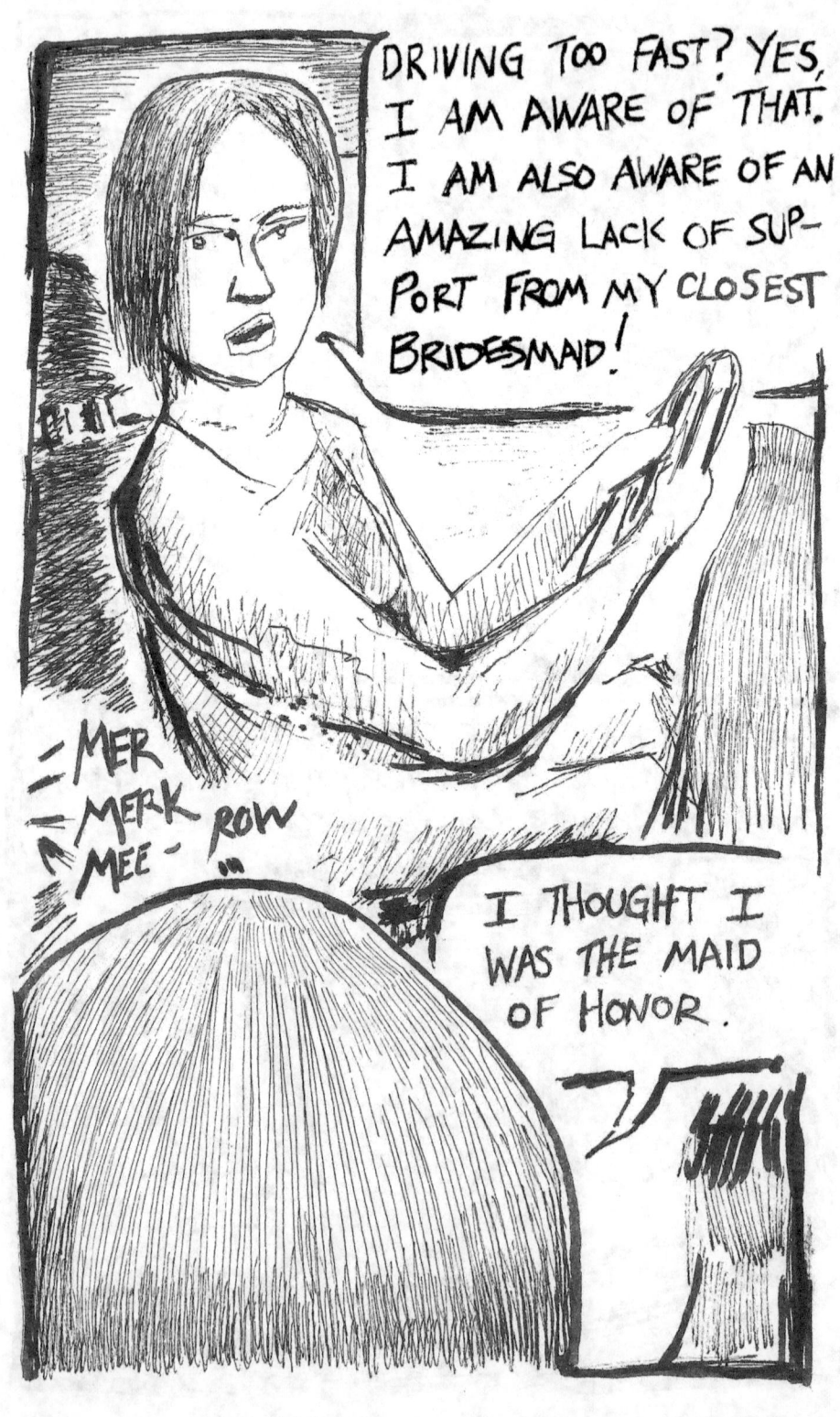

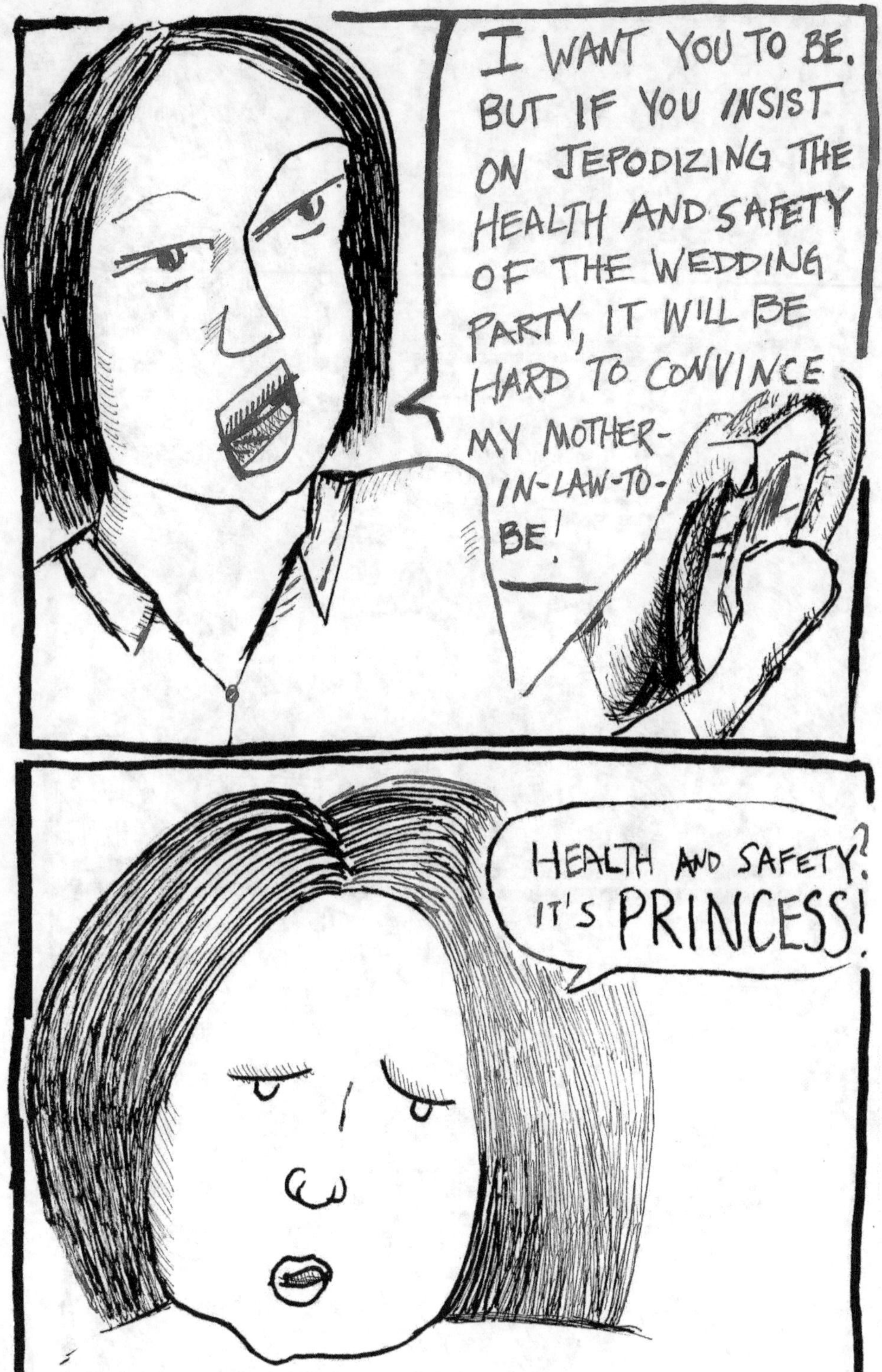
I WANT YOU TO BE. BUT IF YOU INSIST ON JEPODIZING THE HEALTH AND SAFETY OF THE WEDDING PARTY, IT WILL BE HARD TO CONVINCE MY MOTHER-IN-LAW-TO-BE!
HEALTH AND SAFETY? IT'S PRINCESS!

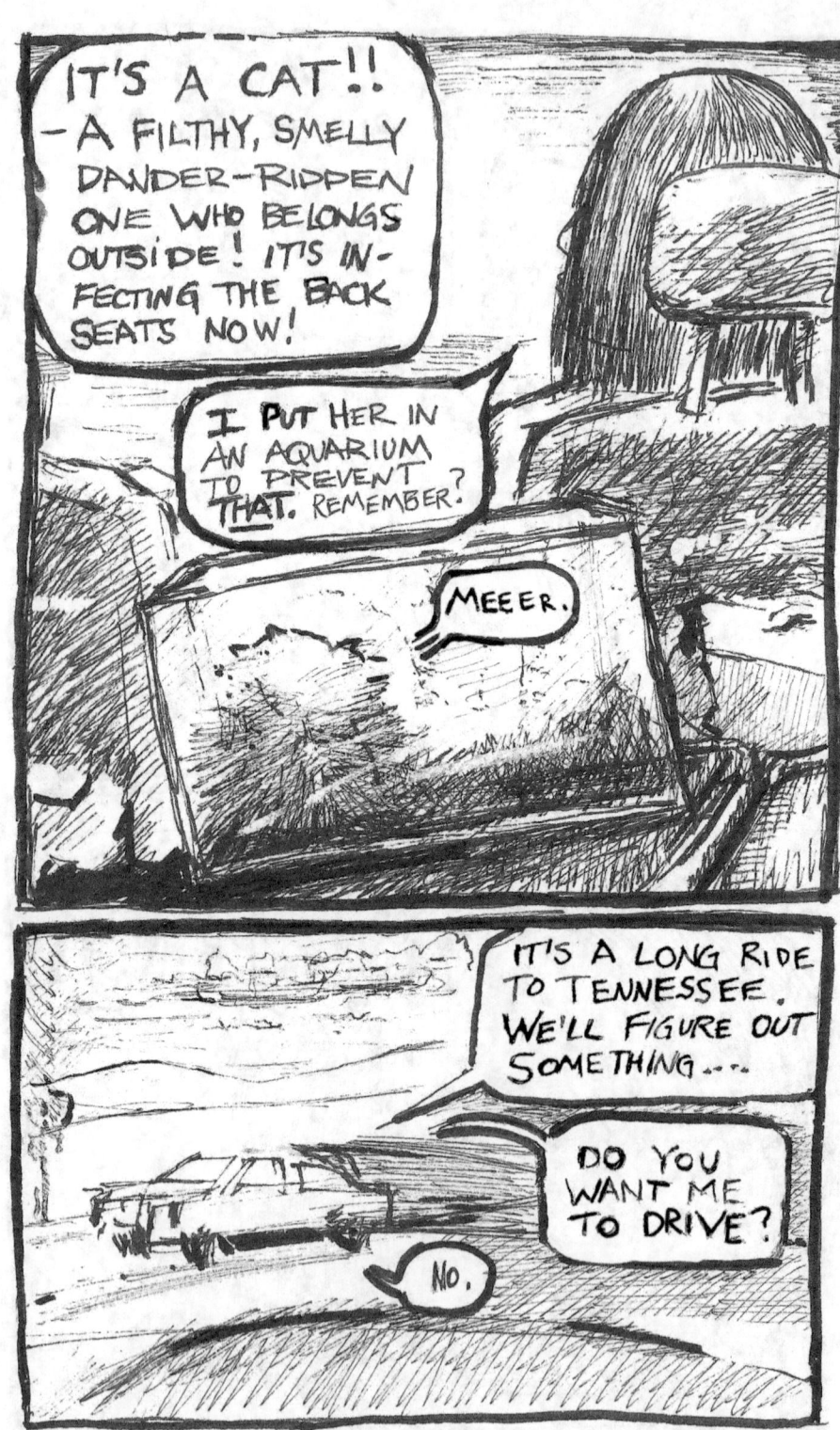

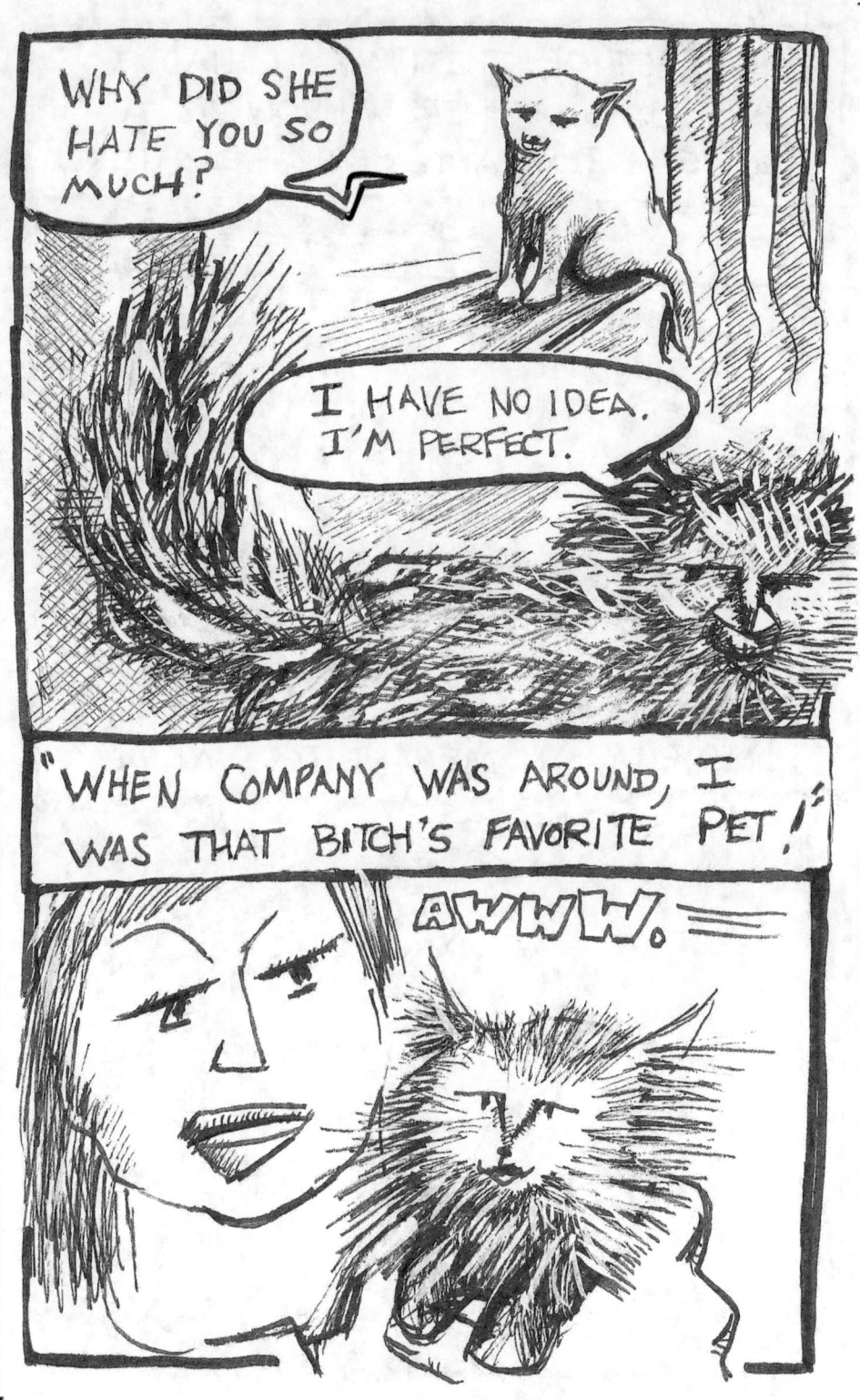

"THE REST OF THE TIME, I HAD TO LIVE OUTSIDE HER WINDOW IN A FLOWER BOX. AFTER THE SEMESTER...

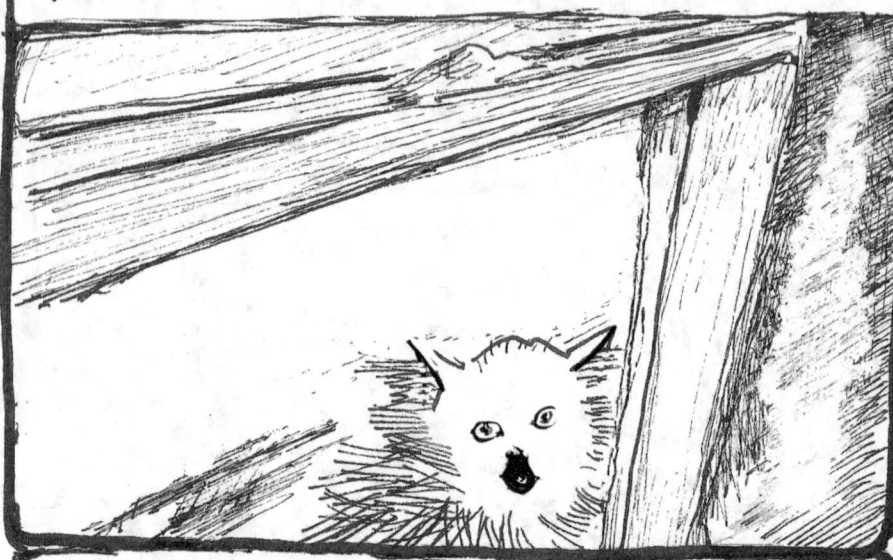

WAS OVER HER NEW ROOMMATE EMILY TOOK PITY ON ME AND TOOK ME IN."

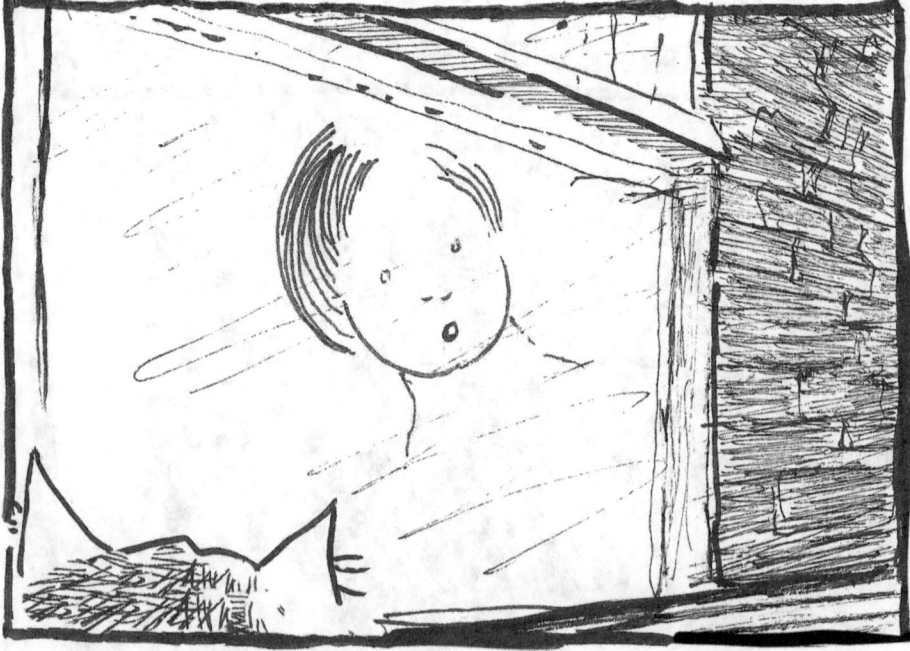

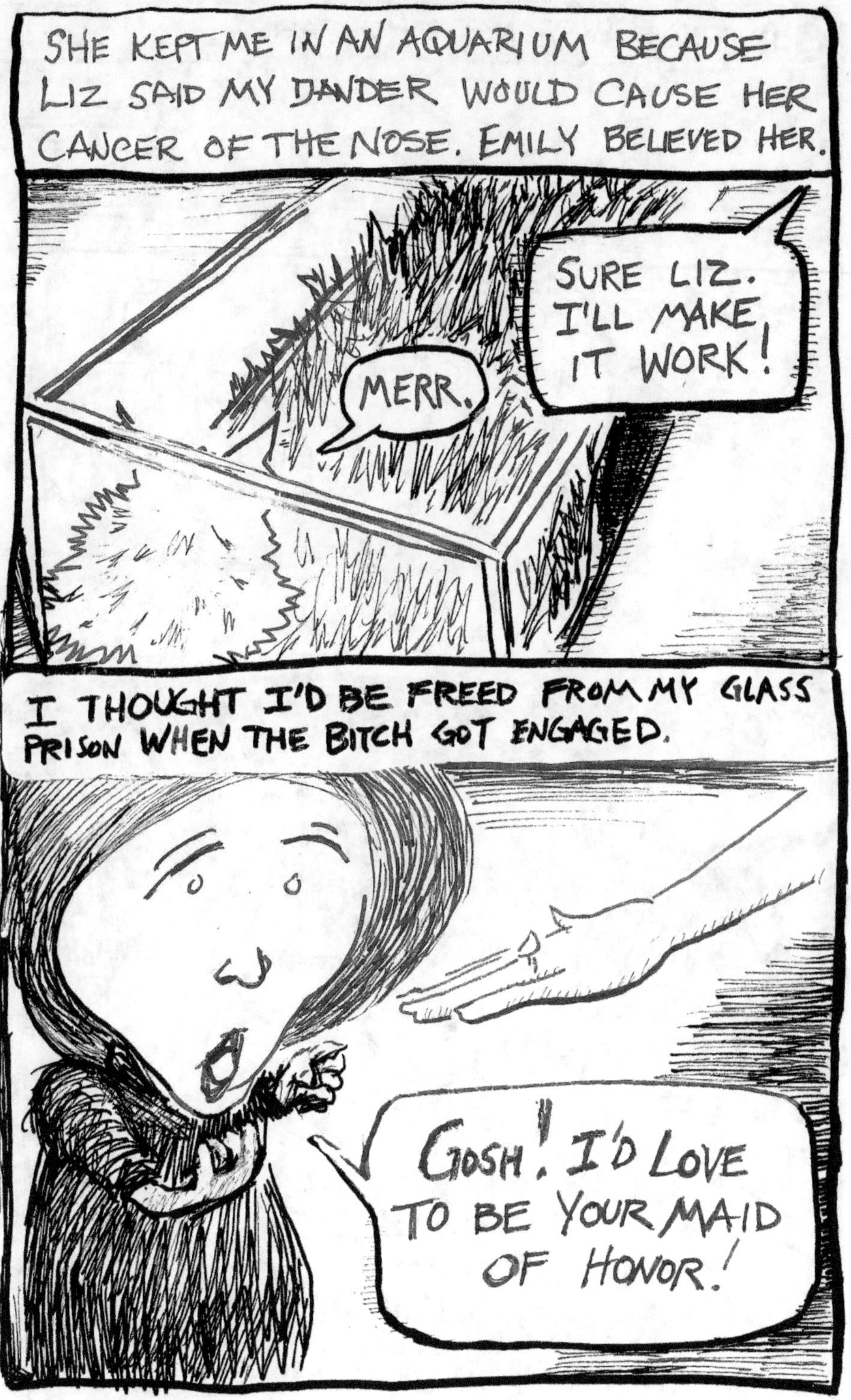
SHE KEPT ME IN AN AQUARIUM BECAUSE LIZ SAID MY DANDER WOULD CAUSE HER CANCER OF THE NOSE. EMILY BELIEVED HER.
SURE LIZ. I'LL MAKE IT WORK!
MERR.
I THOUGHT I'D BE FREED FROM MY GLASS PRISON WHEN THE BITCH GOT ENGAGED.
GOSH! I'D LOVE TO BE YOUR MAID OF HONOR!

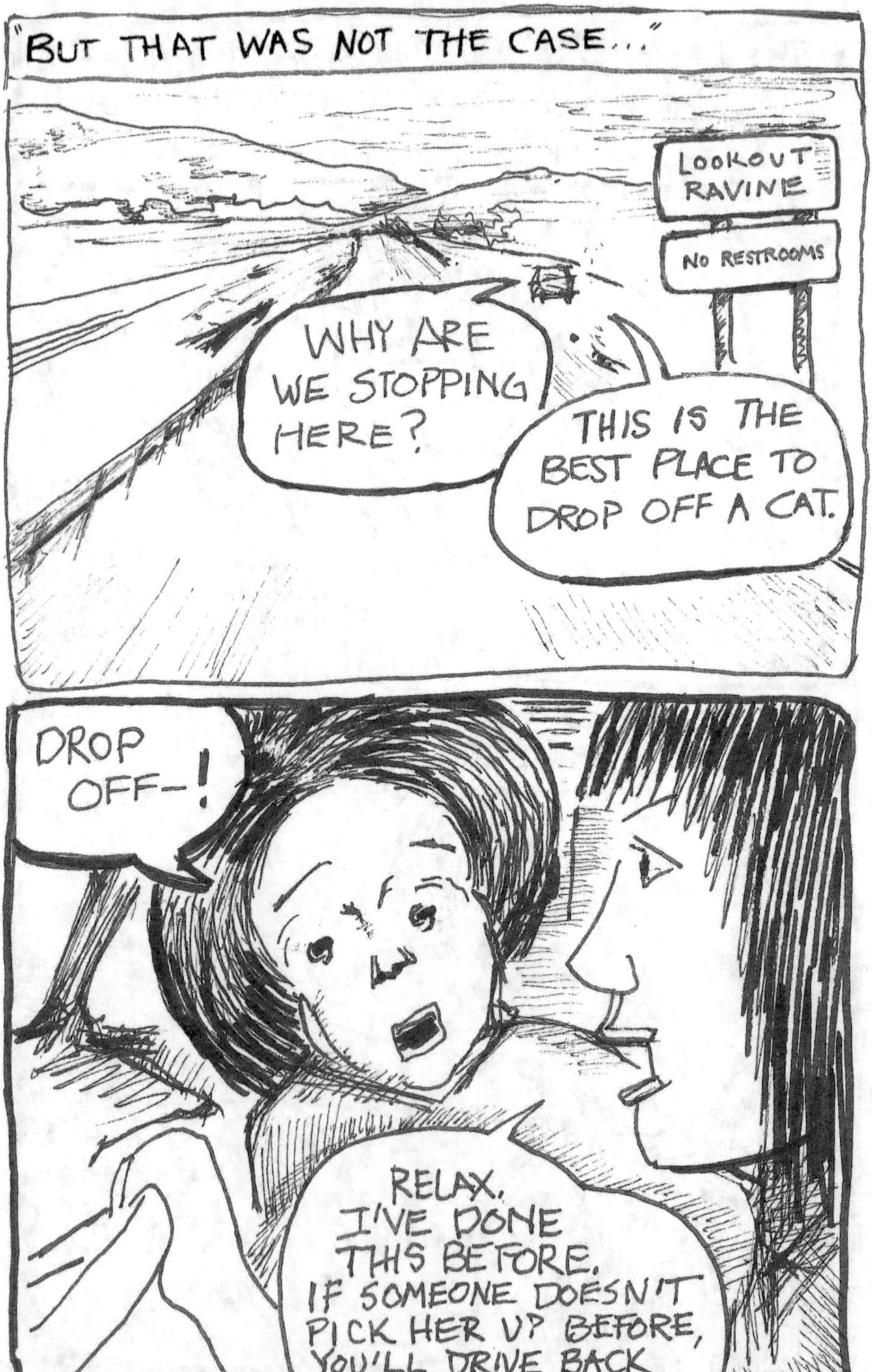
"BUT THAT WAS NOT THE CASE..."
LOOKOUT RAVINE
NO RESTROOMS
WHY ARE WE STOPPING HERE?
THIS IS THE BEST PLACE TO DROP OFF A CAT.
DROP OFF-!
RELAX. I'VE DONE THIS BEFORE. IF SOMEONE DOESN'T PICK HER UP BEFORE, YOU'LL DRIVE BACK AND GET HER.

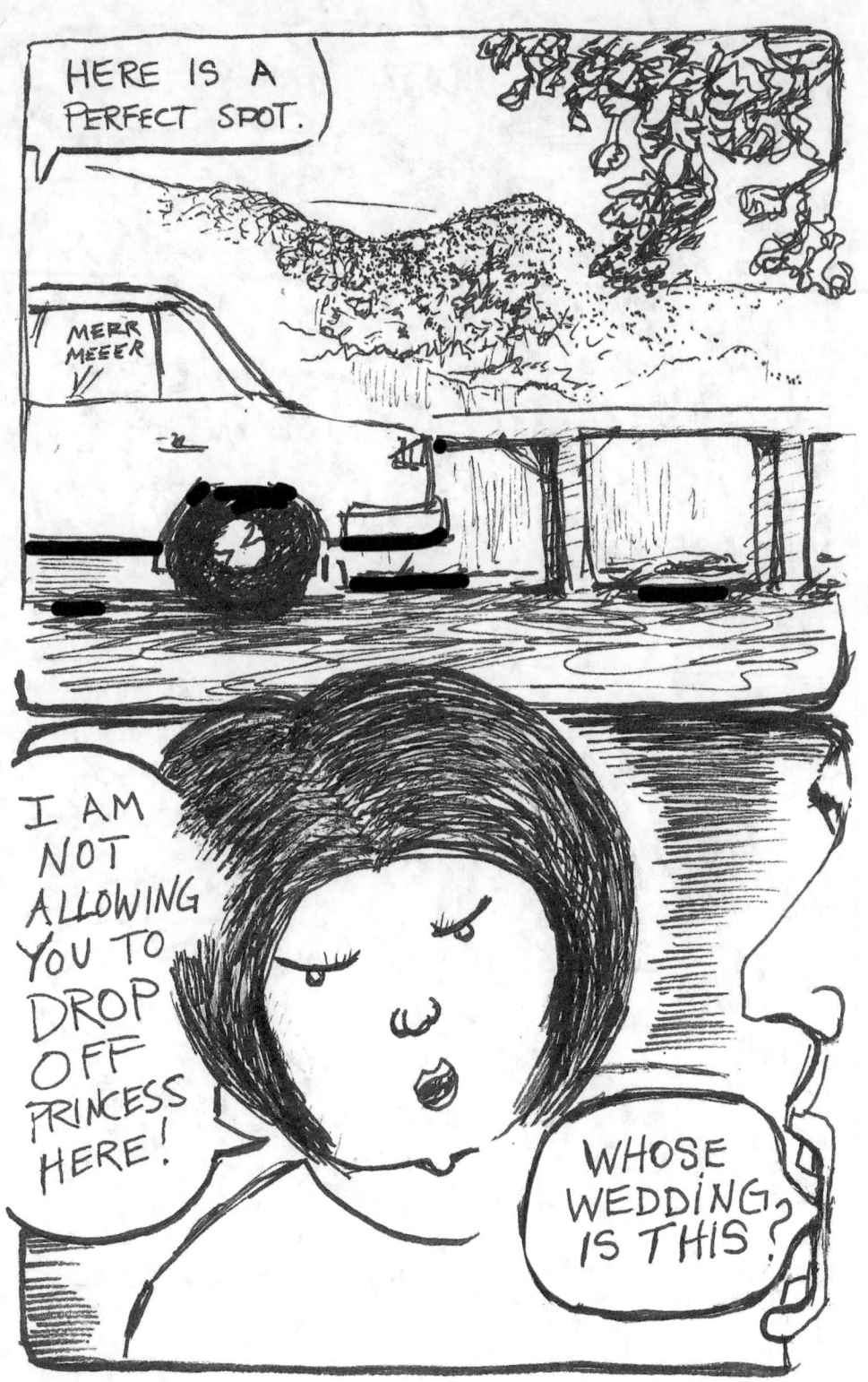

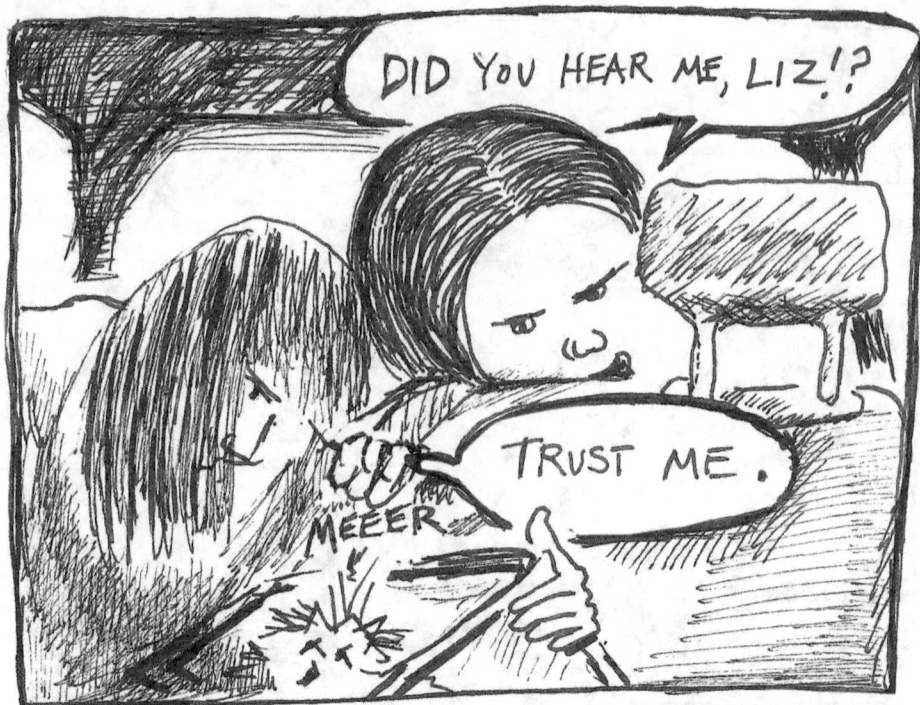

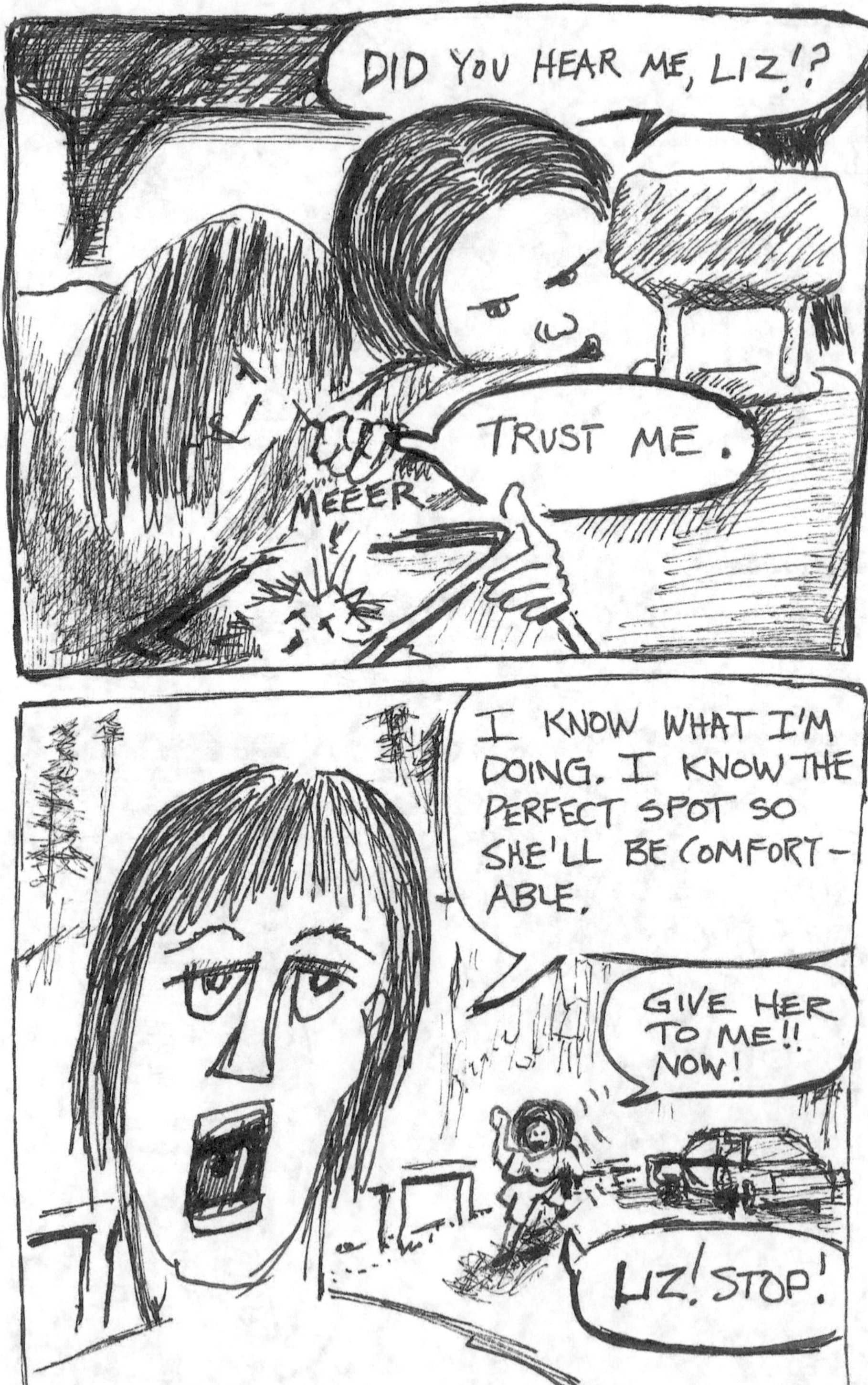

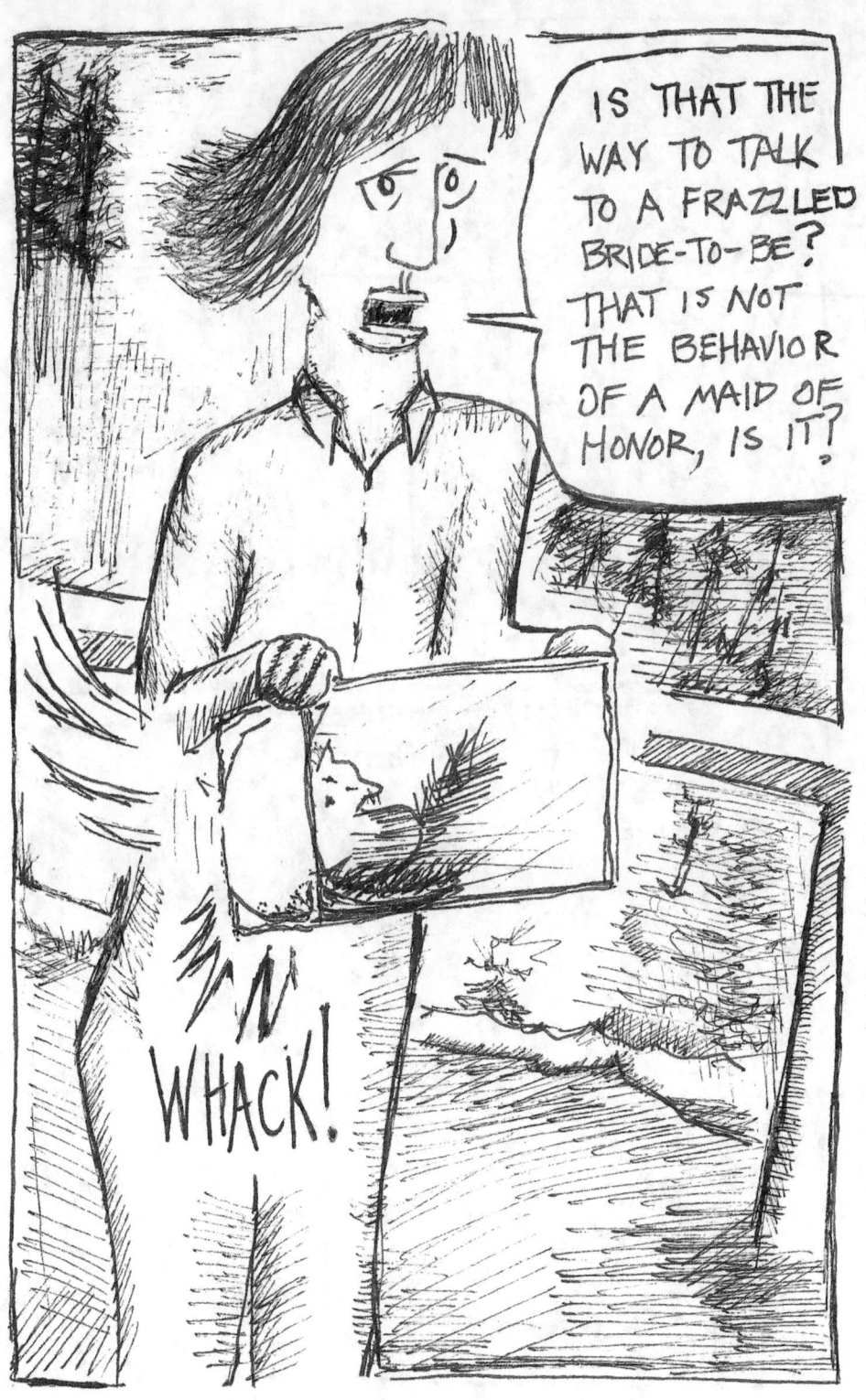

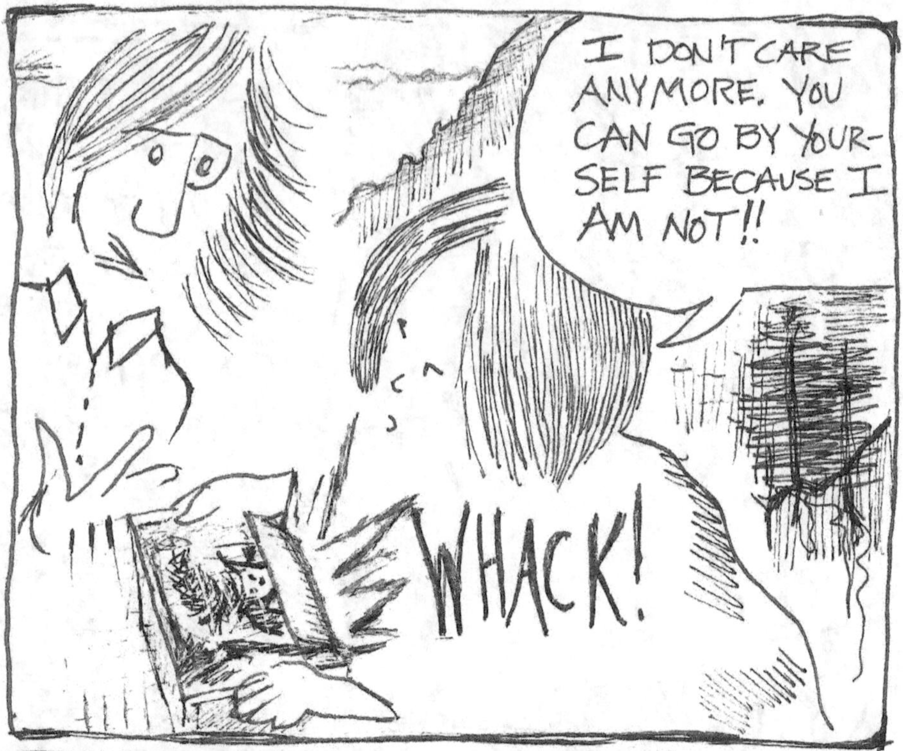
I DON'T CARE ANYMORE. YOU CAN GO BY YOURSELF BECAUSE I AM NOT!!
WHACK!

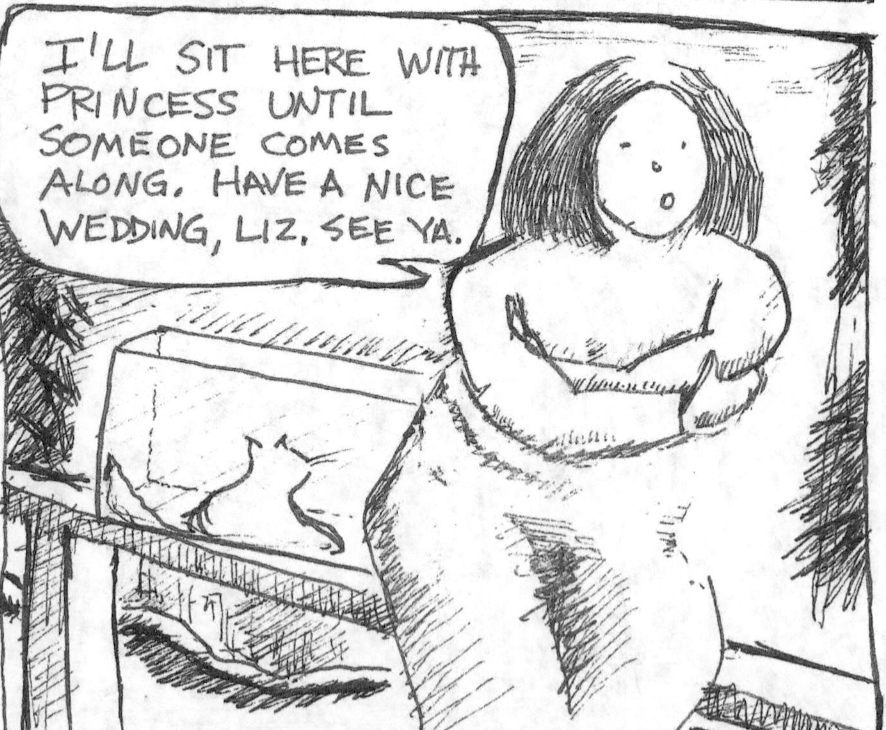
I'LL SIT HERE WITH PRINCESS UNTIL SOMEONE COMES ALONG. HAVE A NICE WEDDING, LIZ. SEE YA.

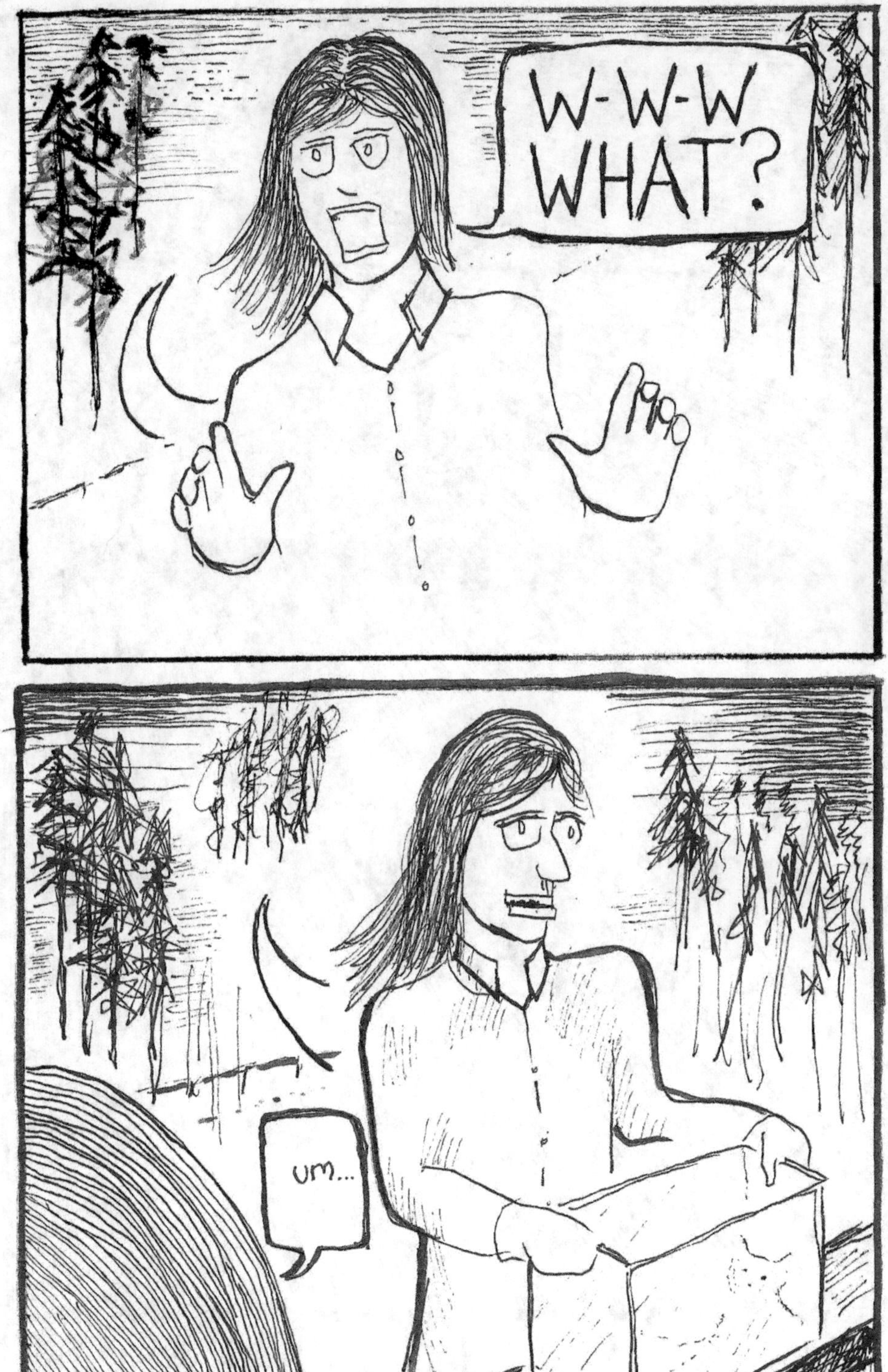
W-W-W WHAT?
UM...

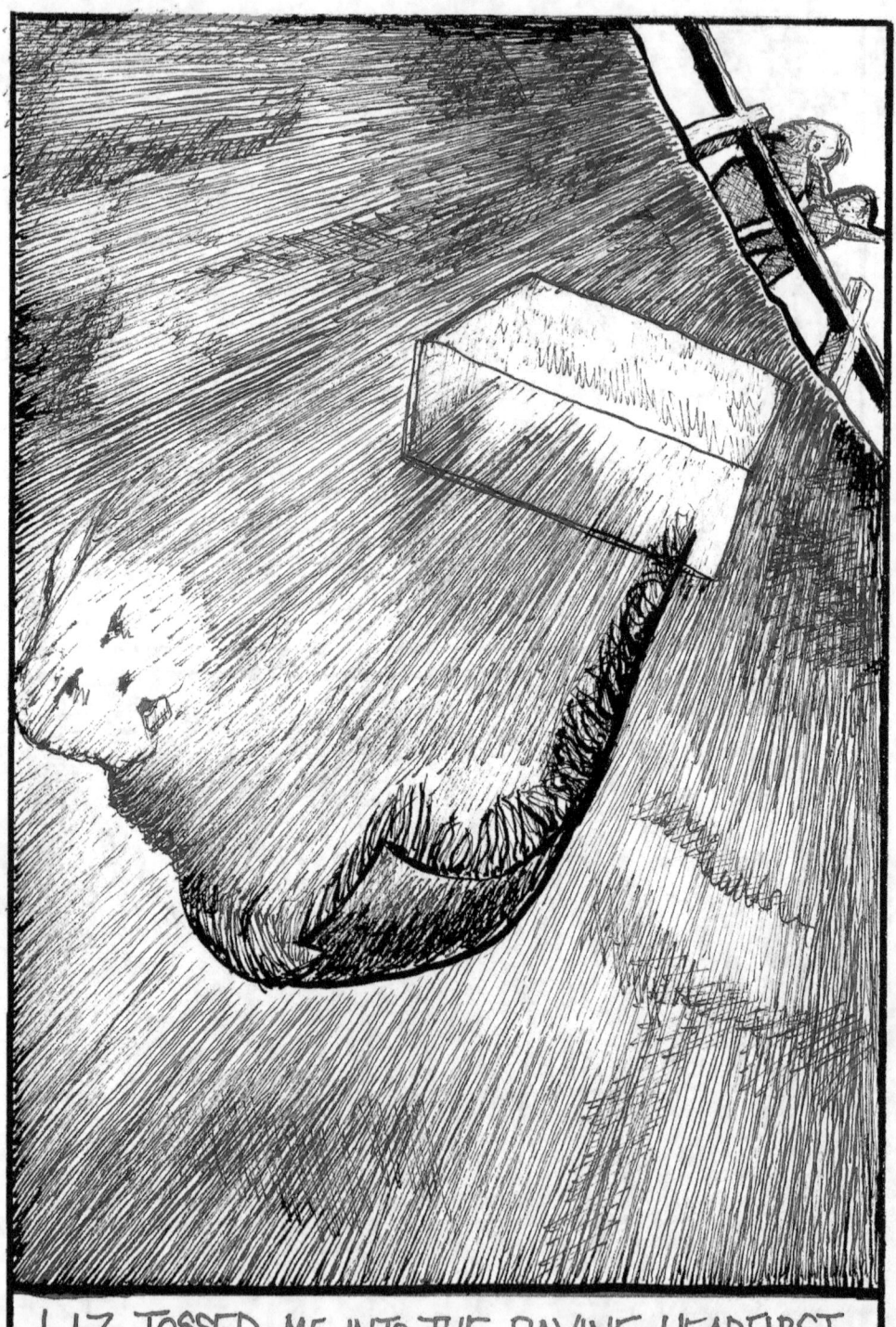

LIZ TOSSED ME INTO THE RAVINE HEADFIRST.

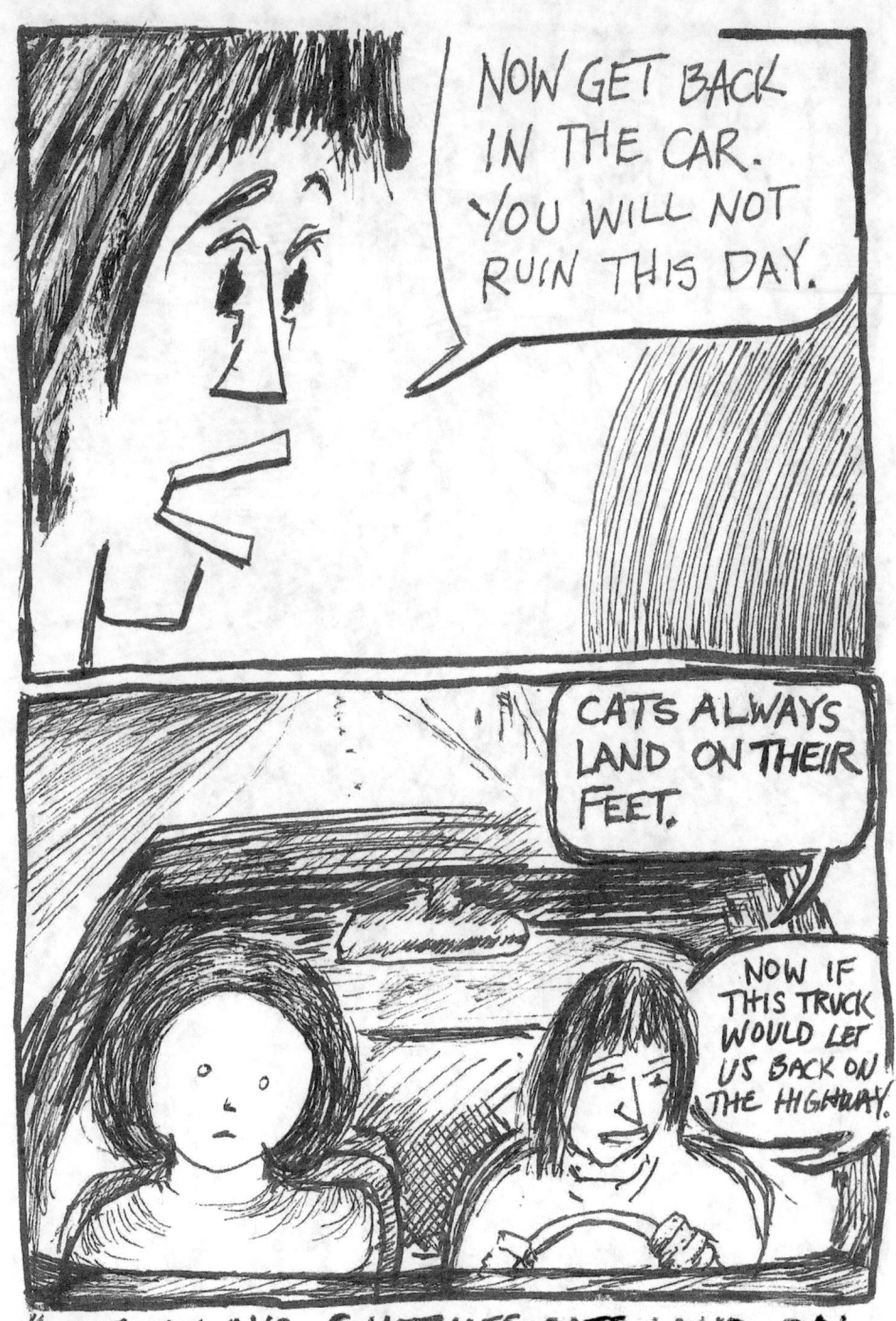

"NOT ALWAYS. SOMETIMES CATS LAND ON THEIR BACKS. BEFORE I DID I HEARD:"

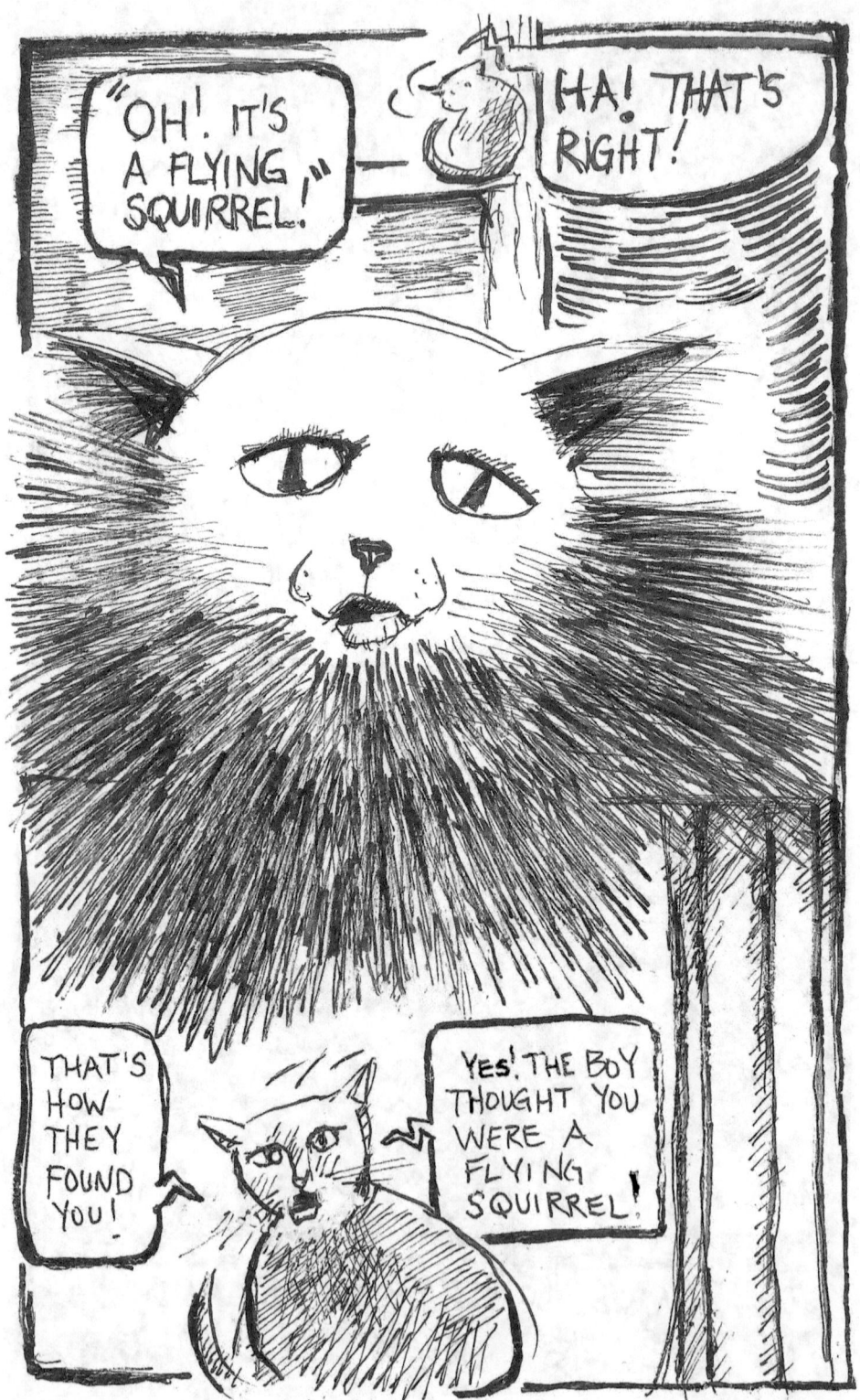

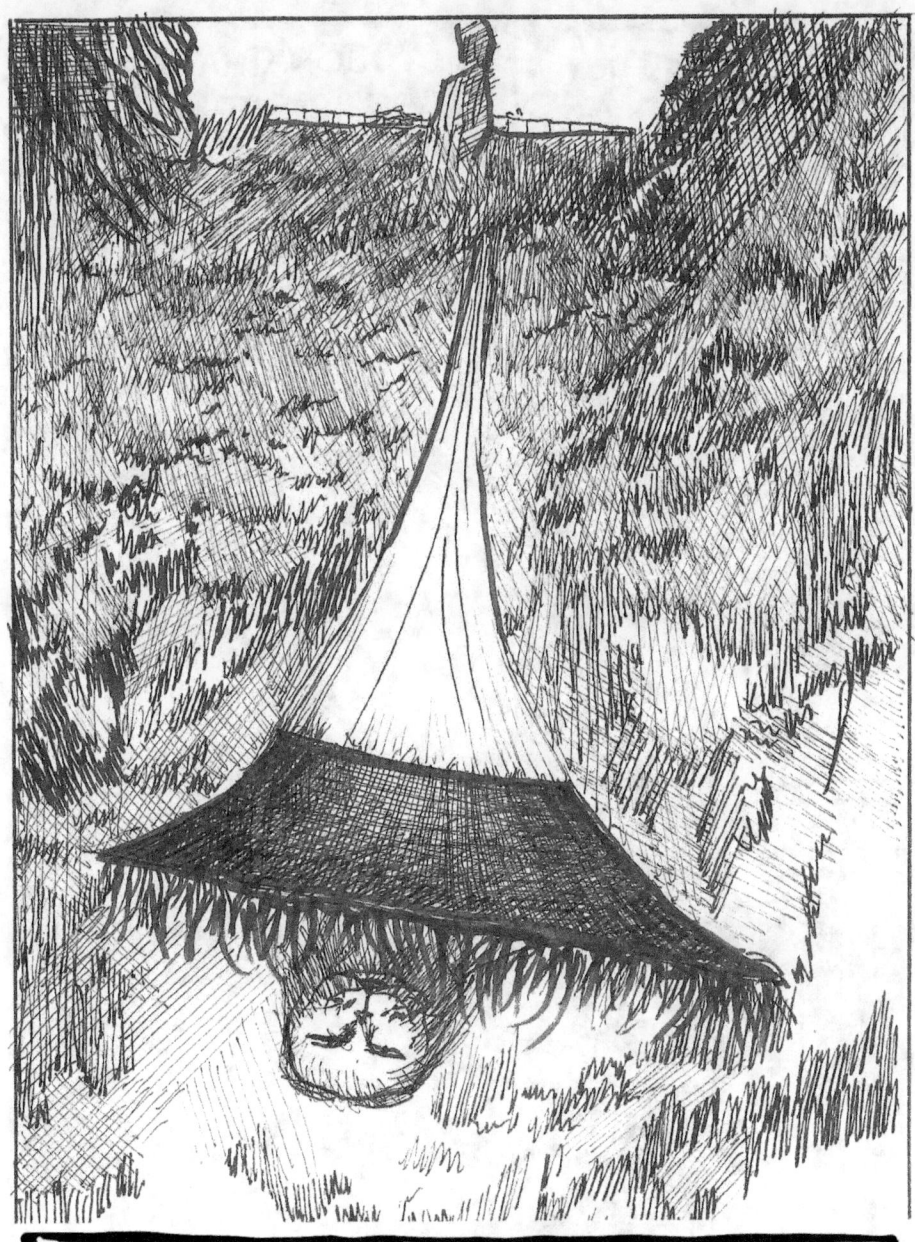

"SO AFEARED WAS I THAT I DUG MY CLAWS INTO THE FAKE GRASS FROM THE AQUARIUM, AND **NOW IT** ACTED AS A GLIDER AS I DESCENDED INTO THE RAVINE."

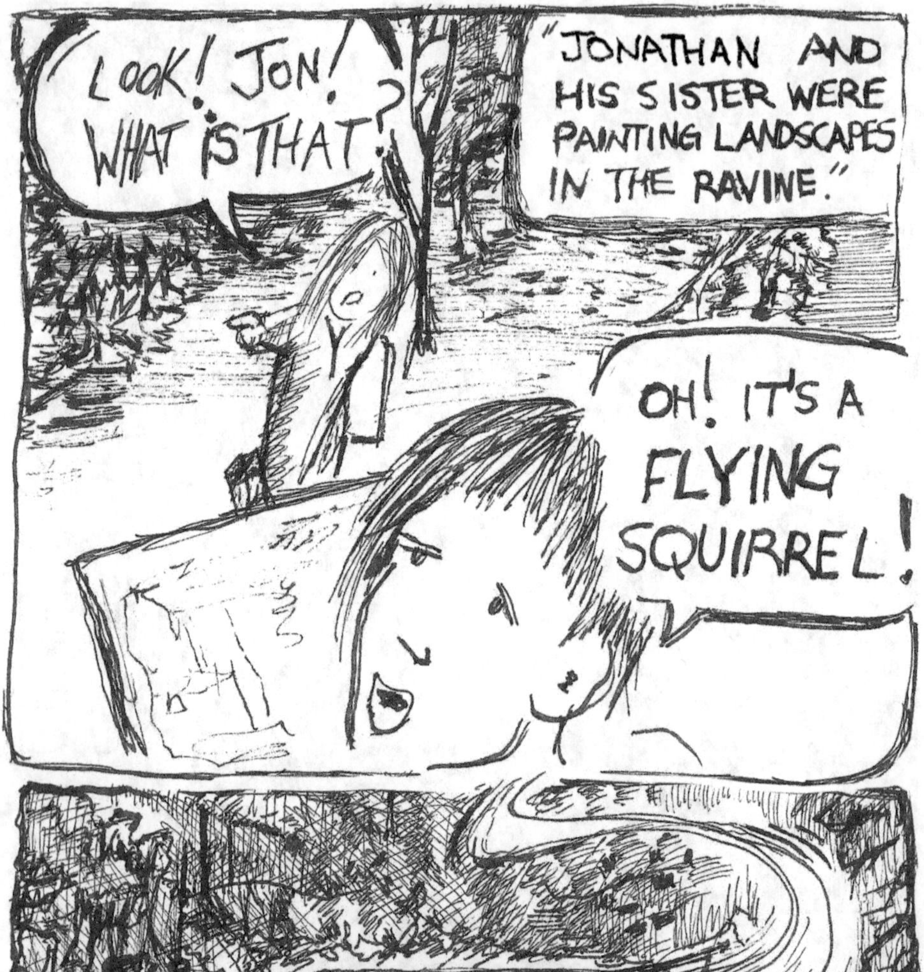

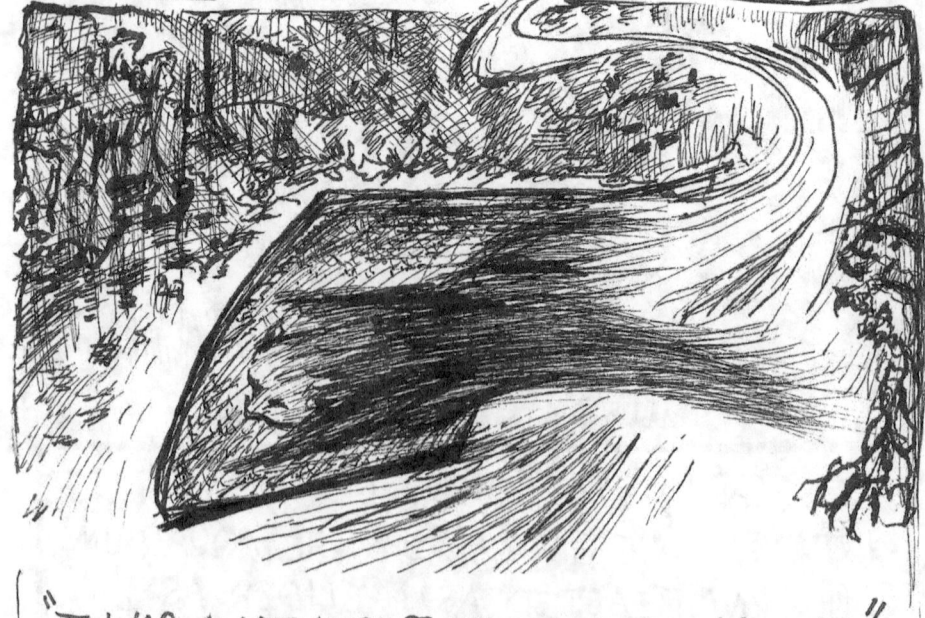

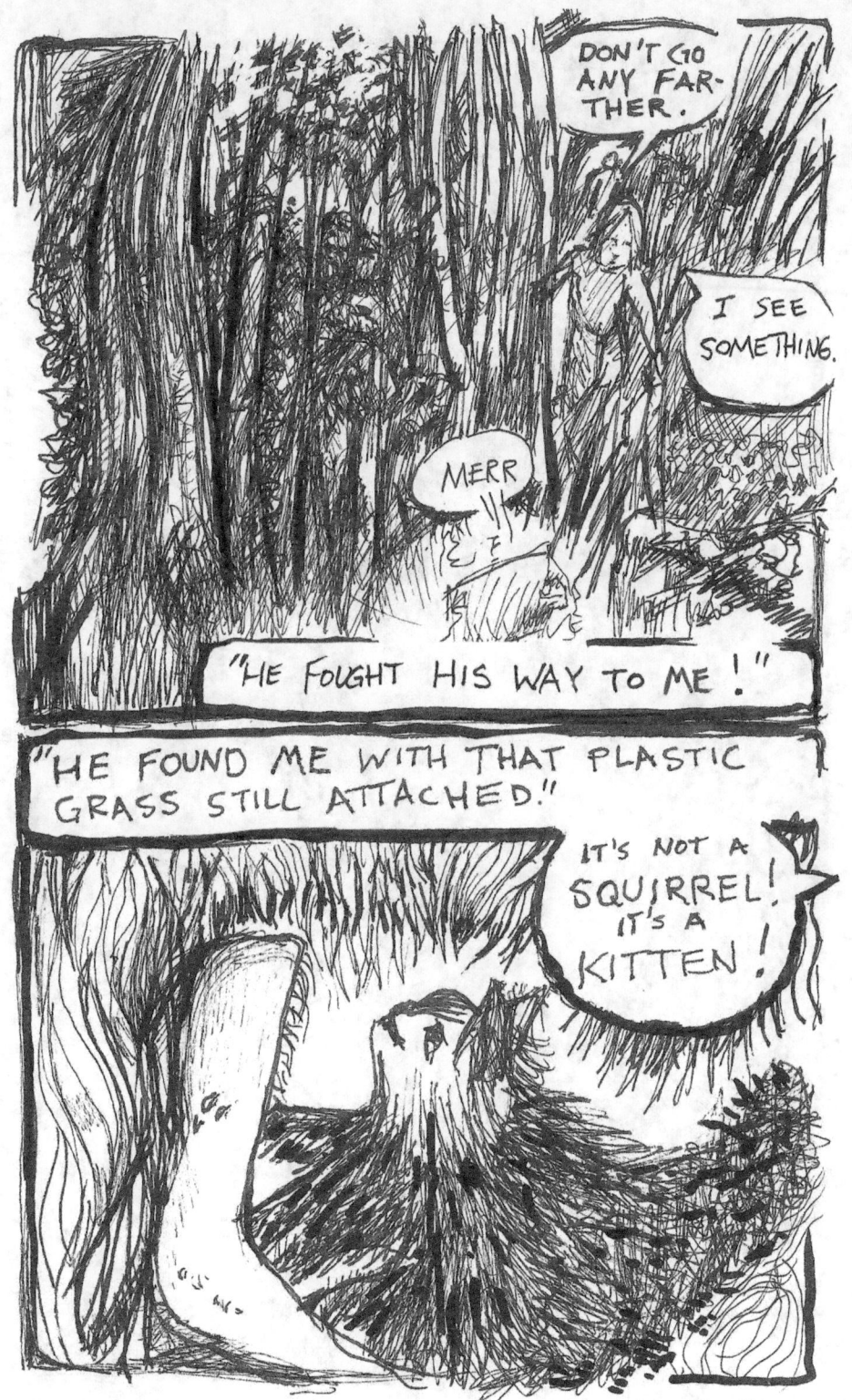

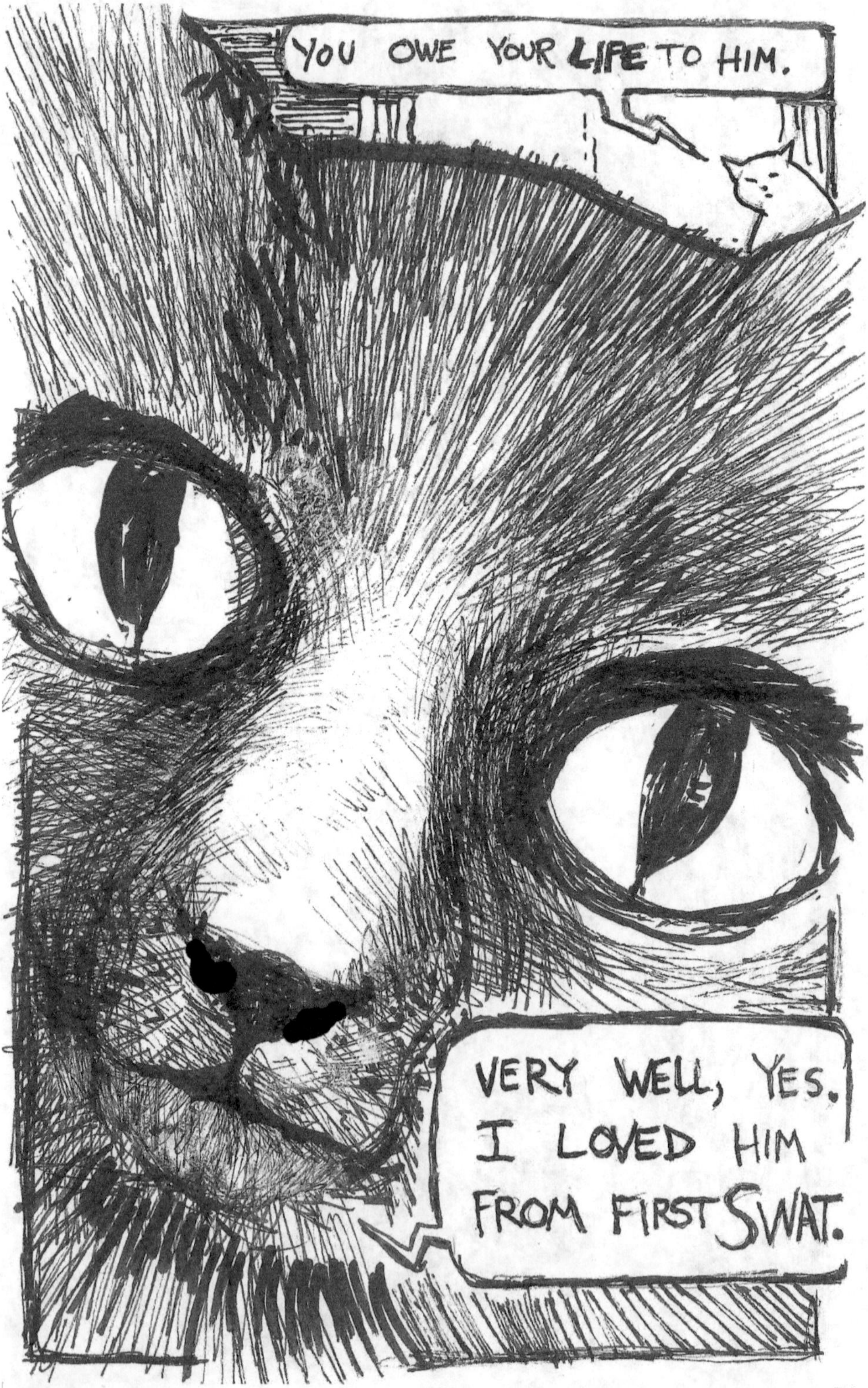
YOU OWE YOUR LIFE TO HIM.
VERY WELL, YES. I LOVED HIM FROM FIRST SWAT.

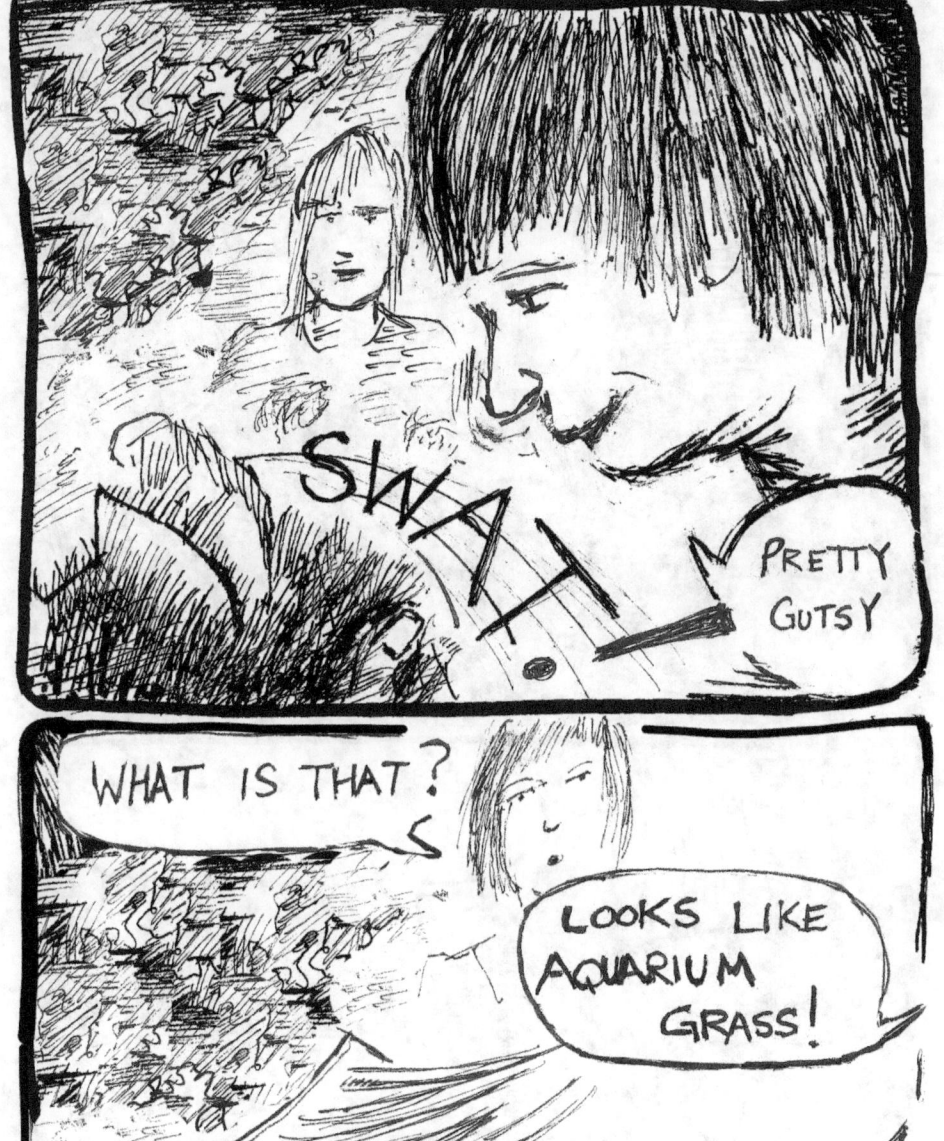

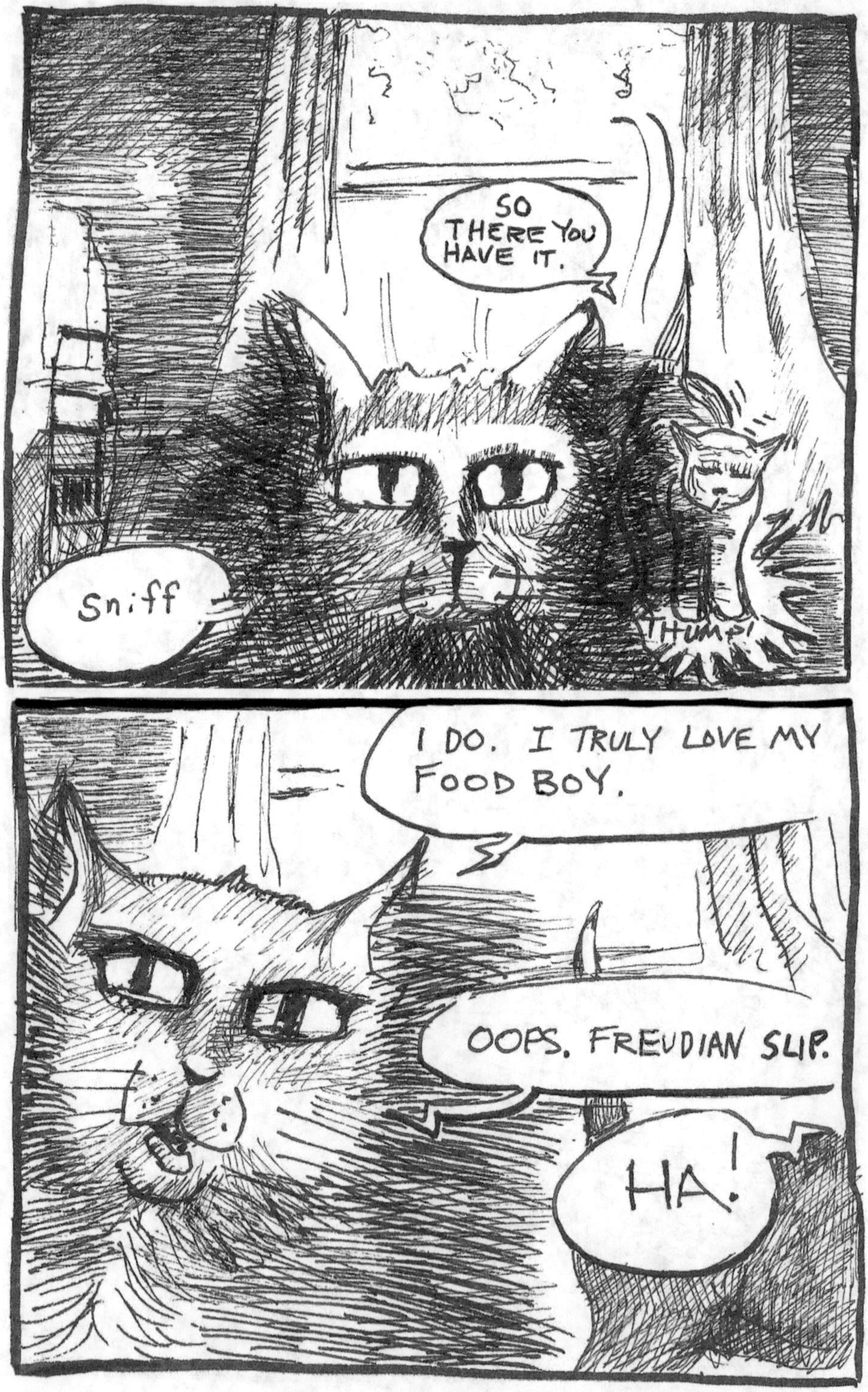
SO THERE YOU HAVE IT.
Sniff
THUMP!
I DO. I TRULY LOVE MY FOOD BOY.
OOPS. FREUDIAN SLIP.
HA!

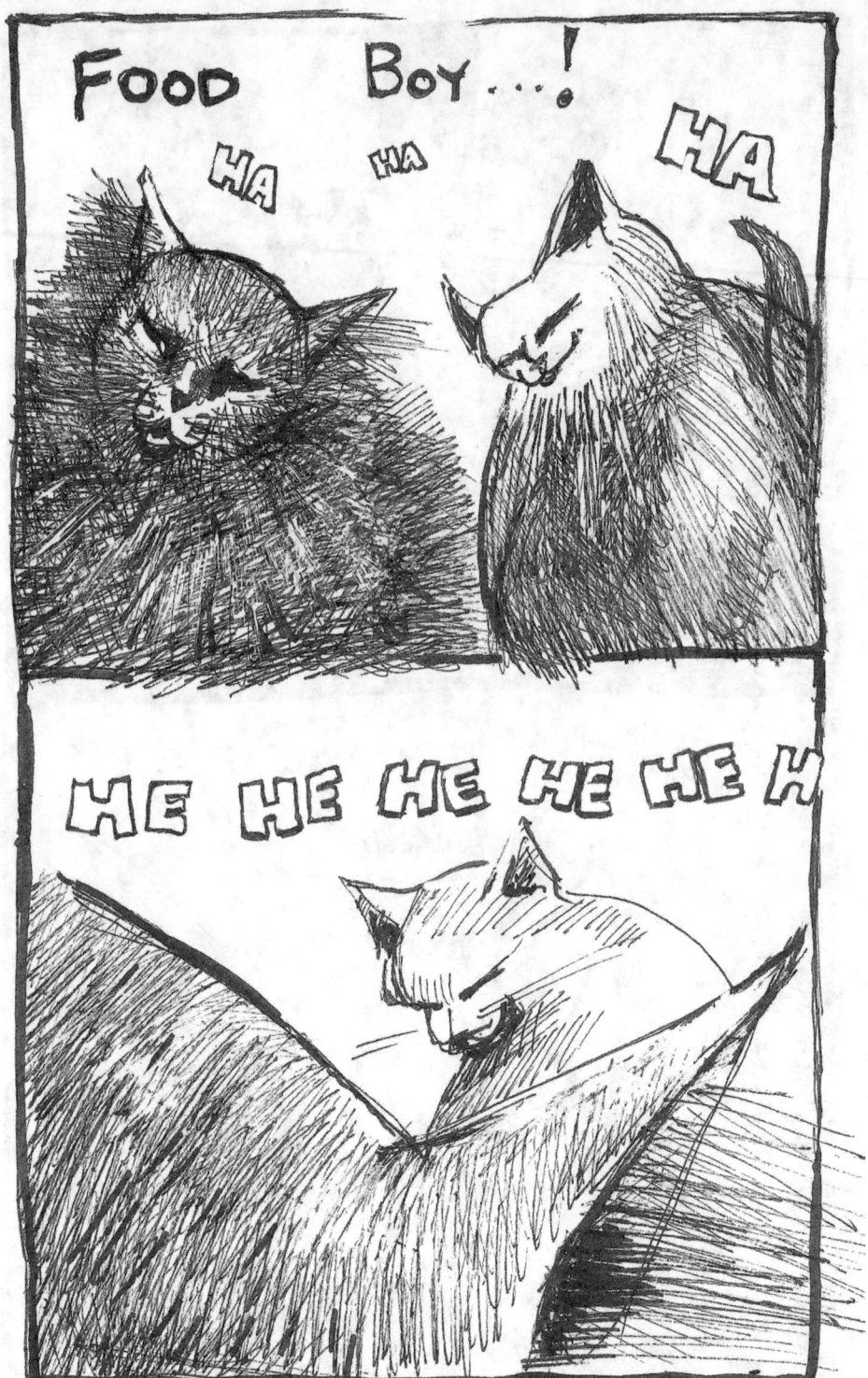

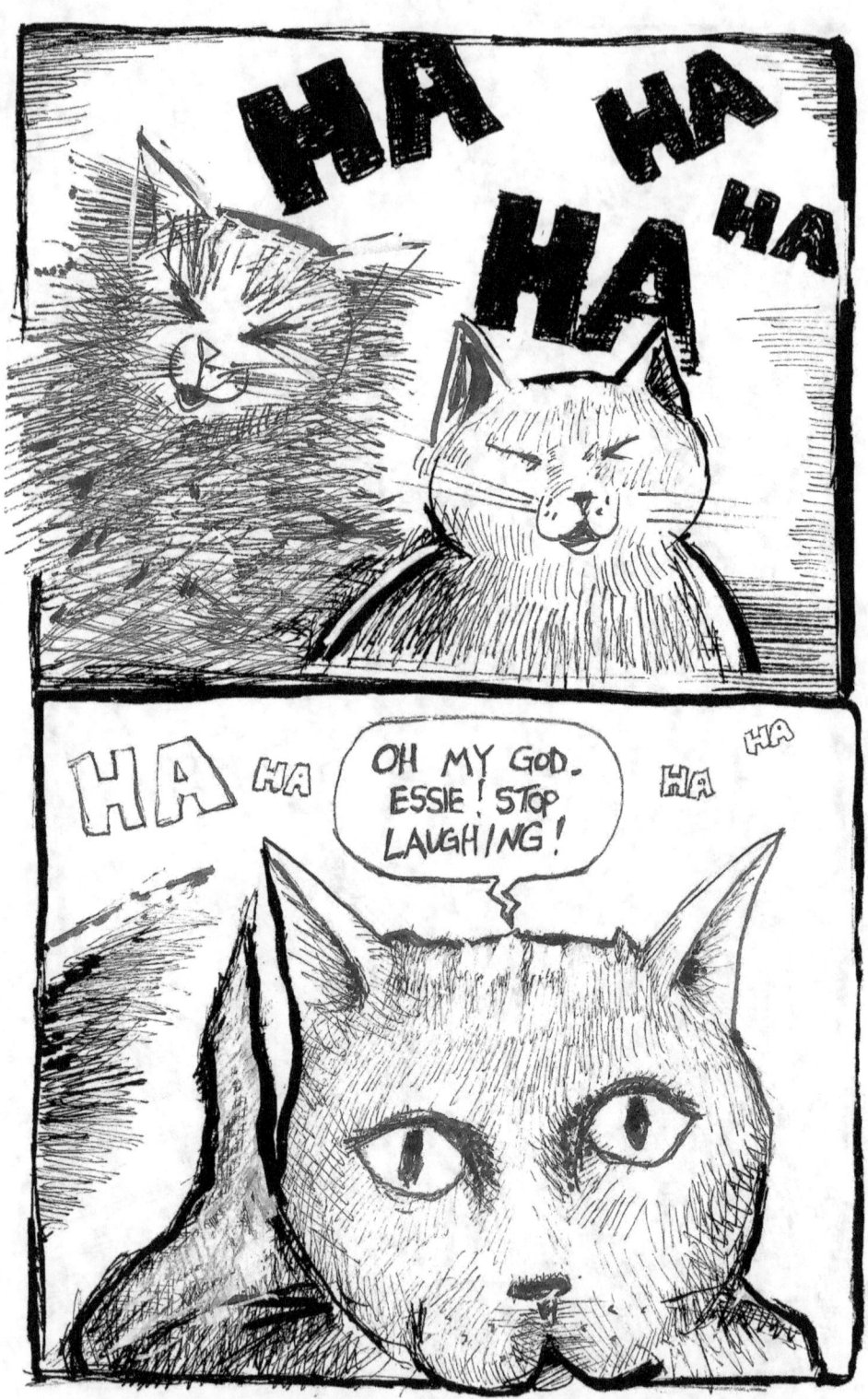

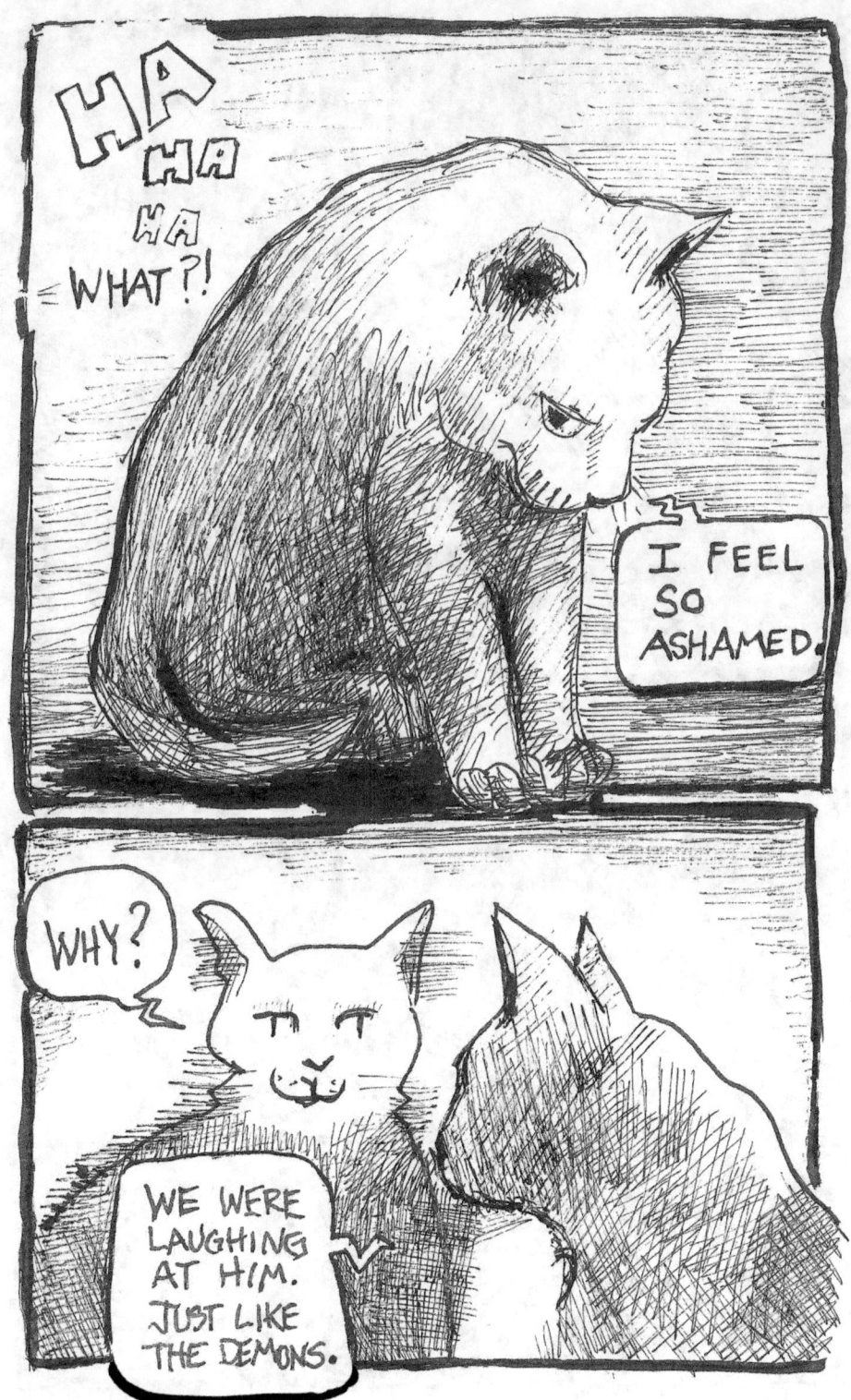

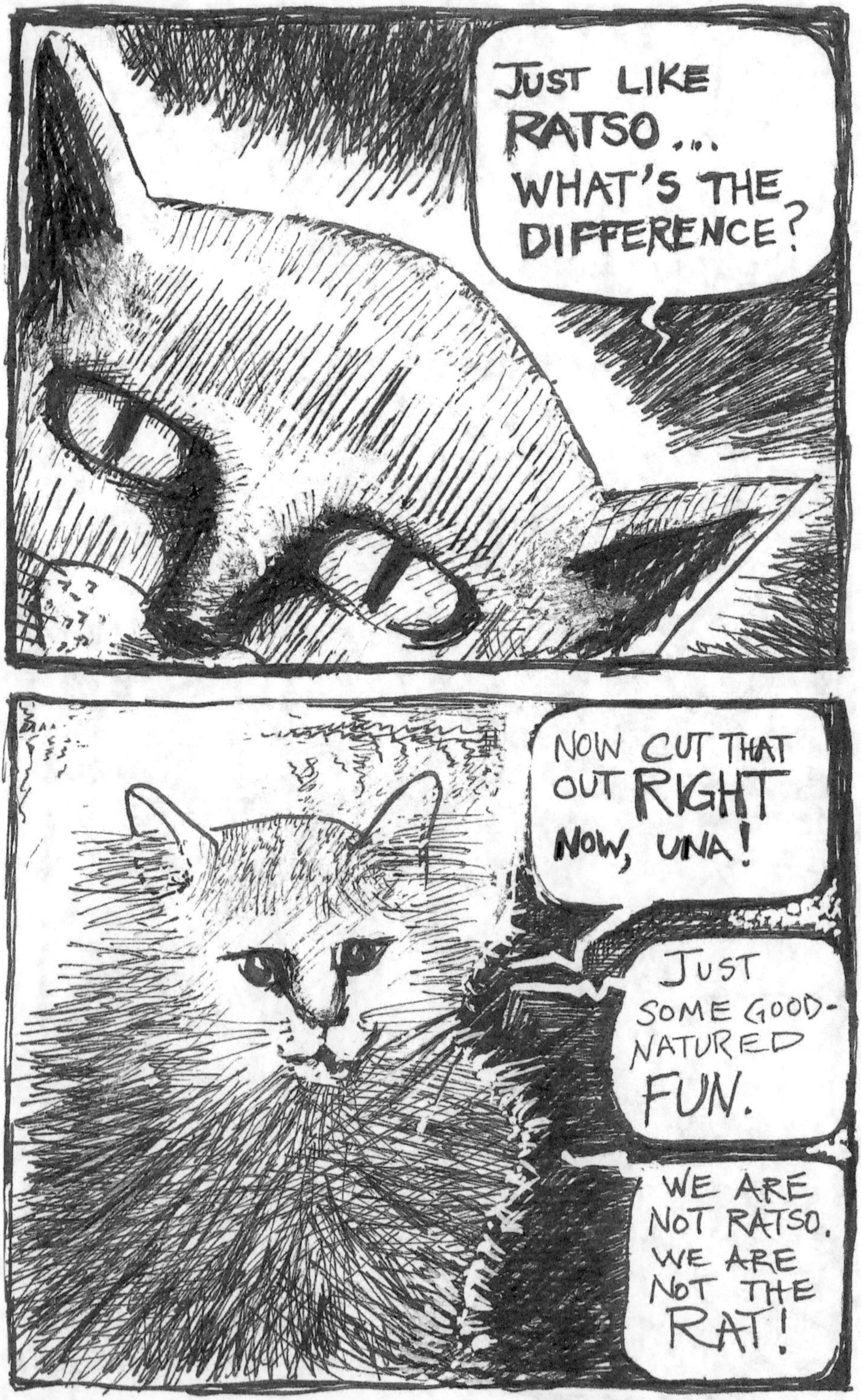
JUST LIKE RATSO.... WHAT'S THE DIFFERENCE?
NOW CUT THAT OUT RIGHT NOW, UNA!
JUST SOME GOOD-NATURED FUN.
WE ARE NOT RATSO. WE ARE NOT THE RAT!

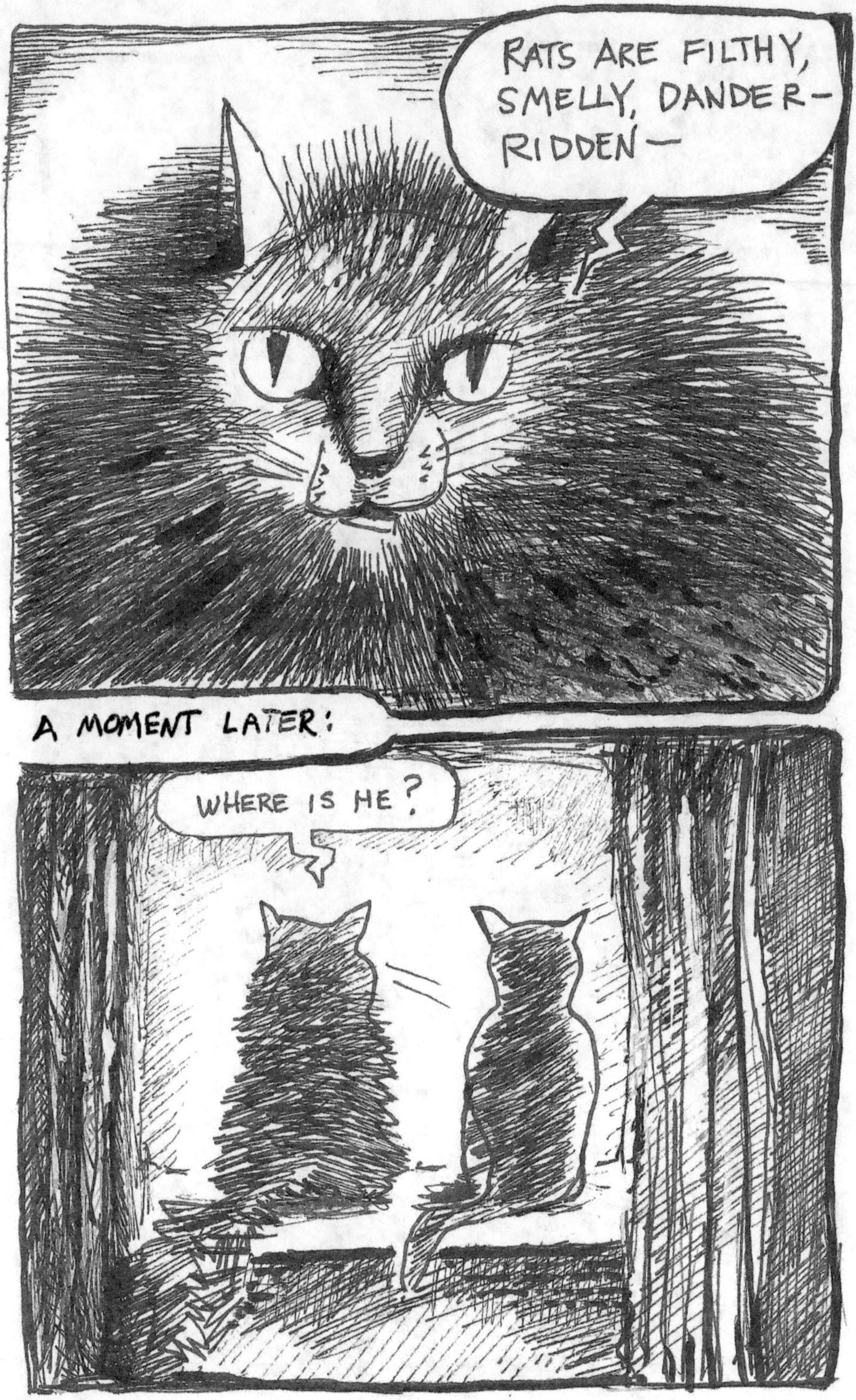

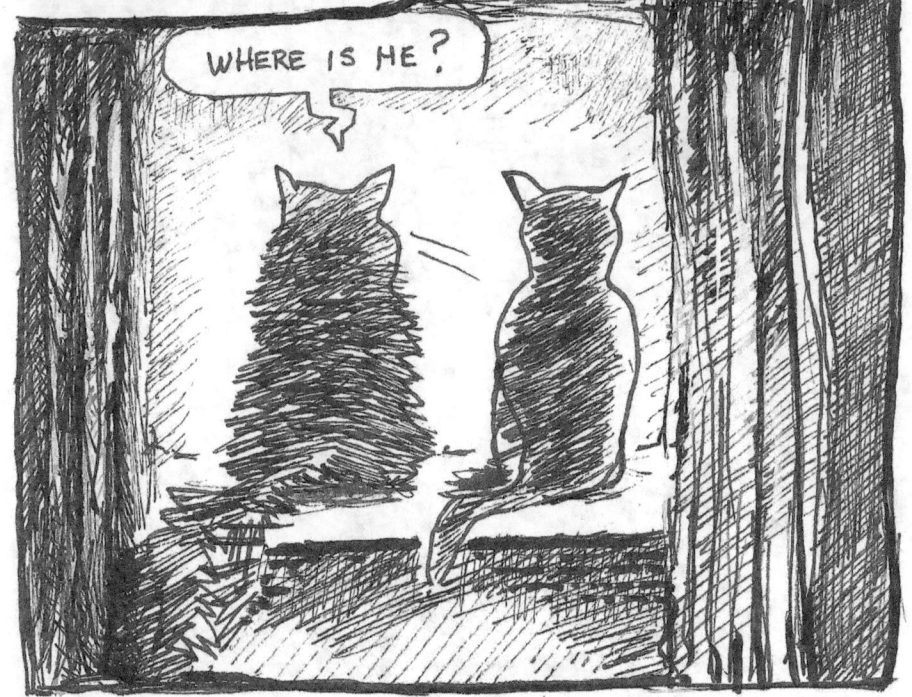

A MOMENT LATER:

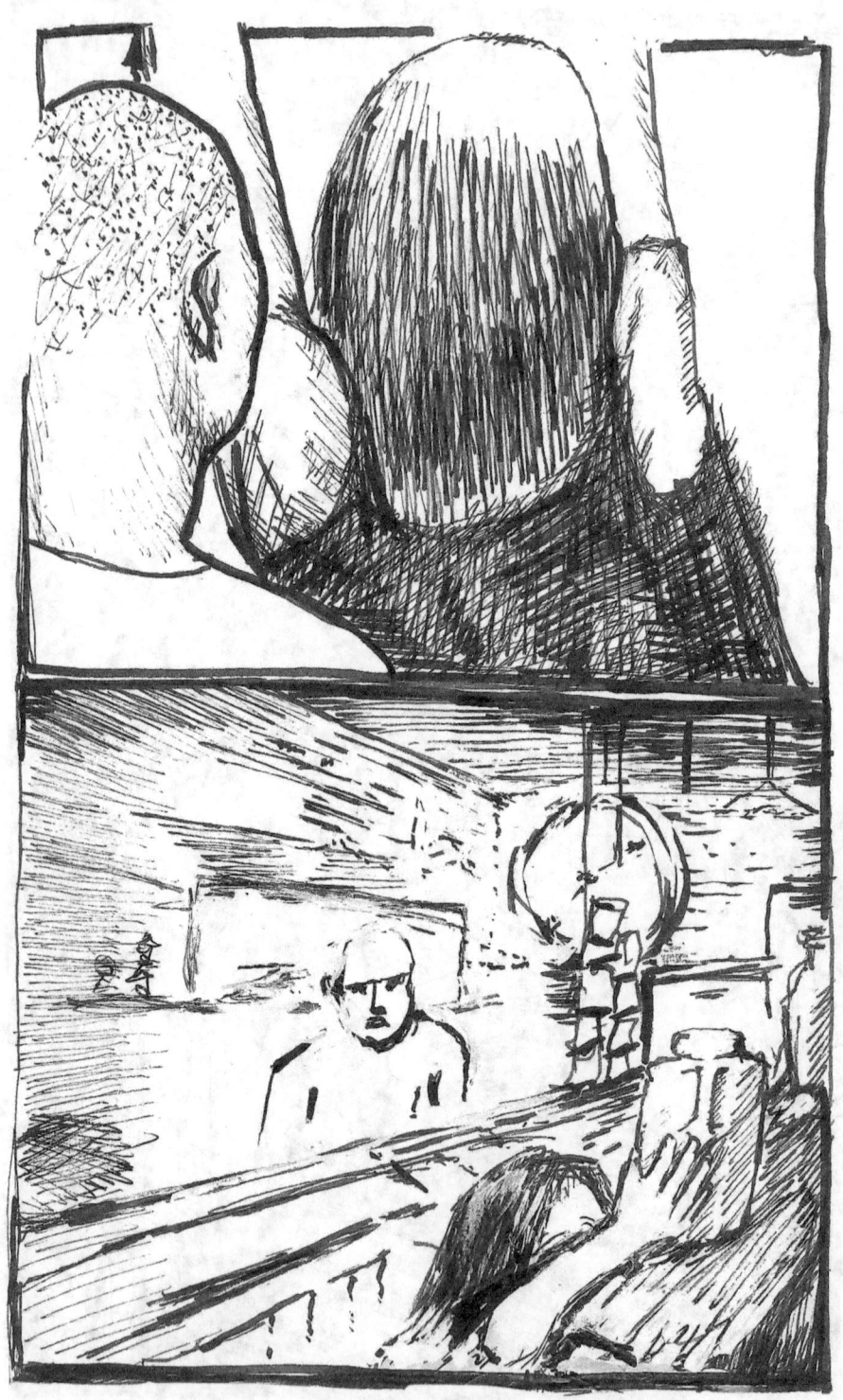

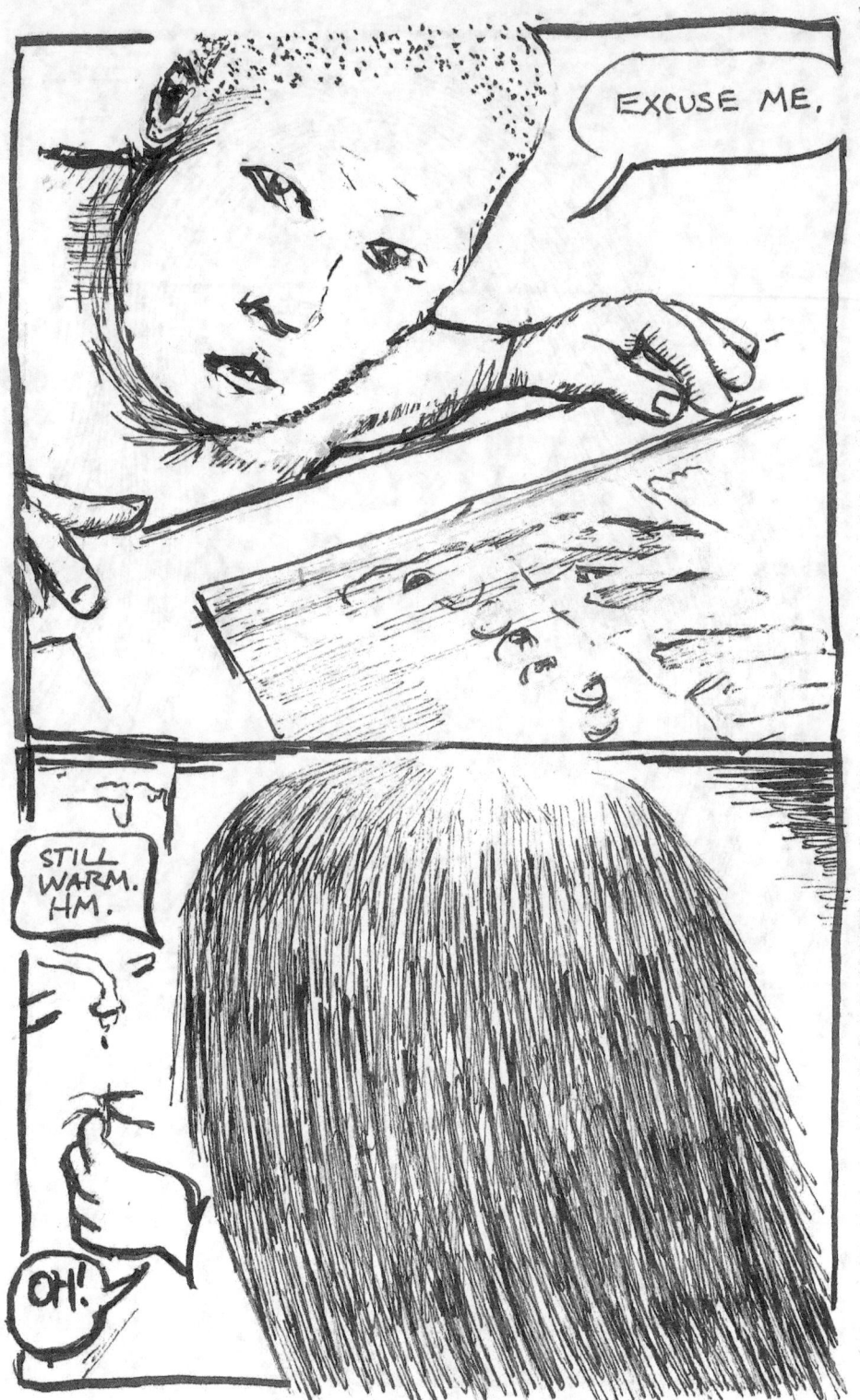

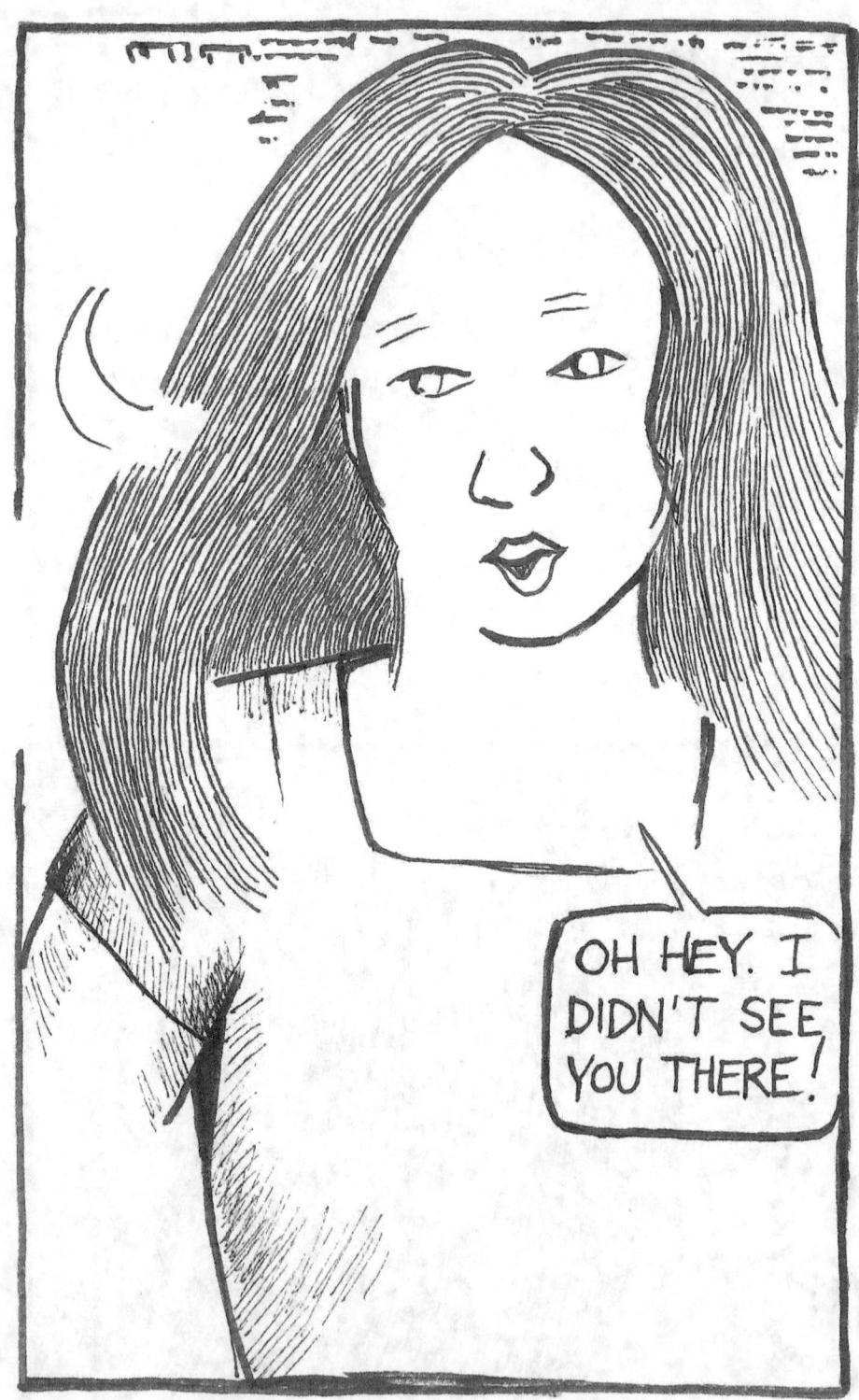

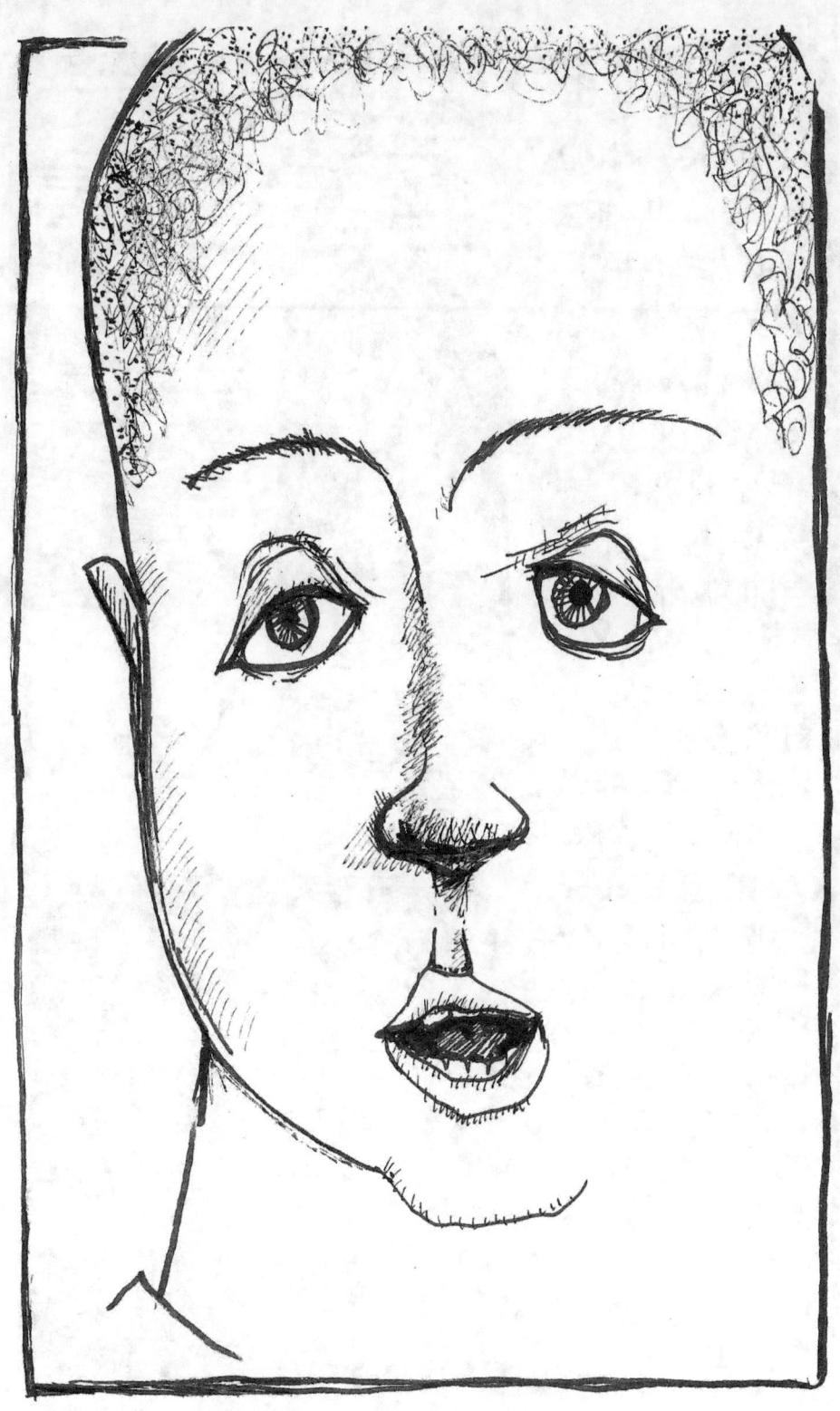

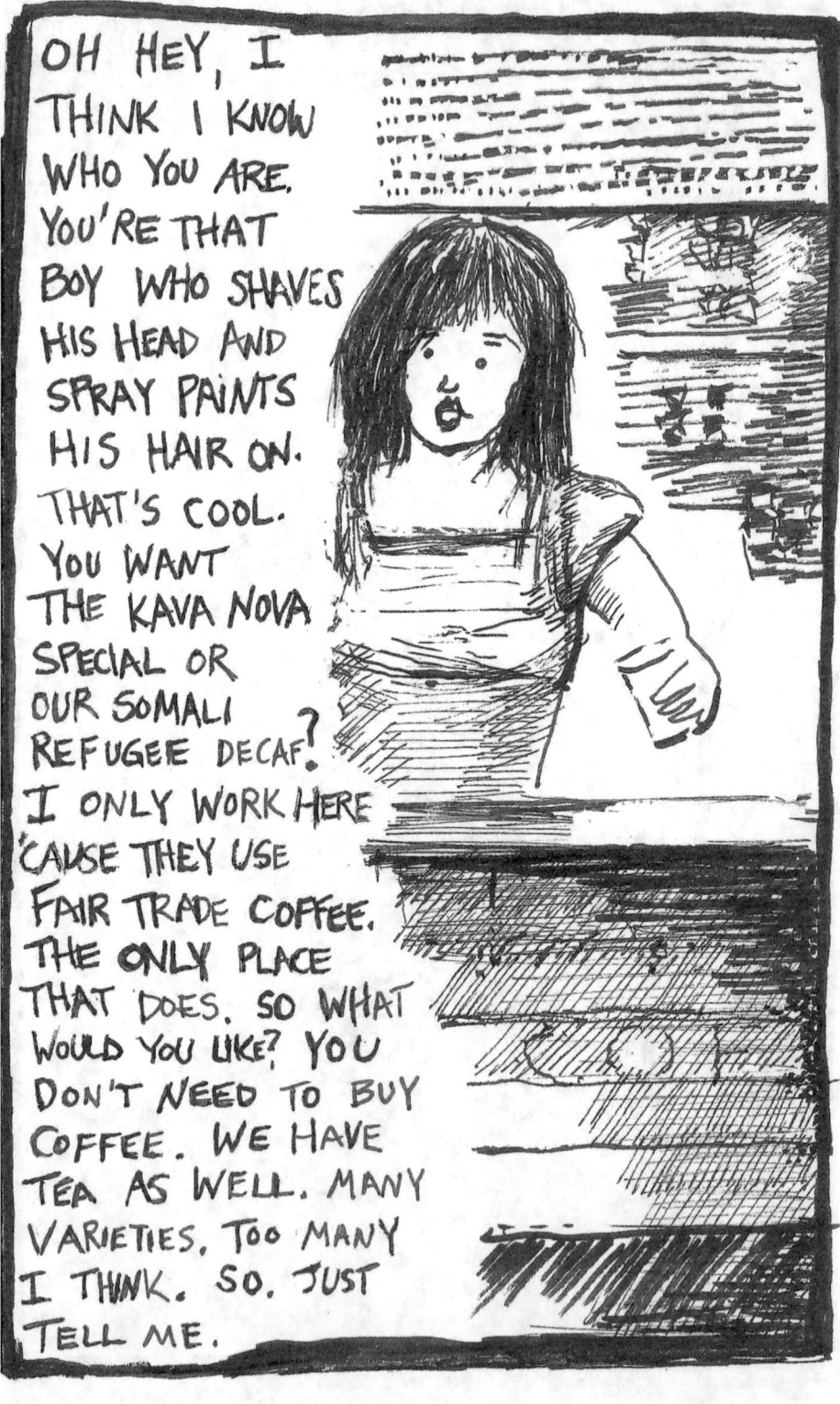

OH HEY, I THINK I KNOW WHO YOU ARE. YOU'RE THAT BOY WHO SHAVES HIS HEAD AND SPRAY PAINTS HIS HAIR ON. THAT'S COOL. YOU WANT THE KAVA NOVA SPECIAL OR OUR SOMALI REFUGEE DECAF? I ONLY WORK HERE 'CAUSE THEY USE FAIR TRADE COFFEE. THE ONLY PLACE THAT DOES. SO WHAT WOULD YOU LIKE? YOU DON'T NEED TO BUY COFFEE. WE HAVE TEA AS WELL. MANY VARIETIES, TOO MANY I THINK. SO. JUST TELL ME.

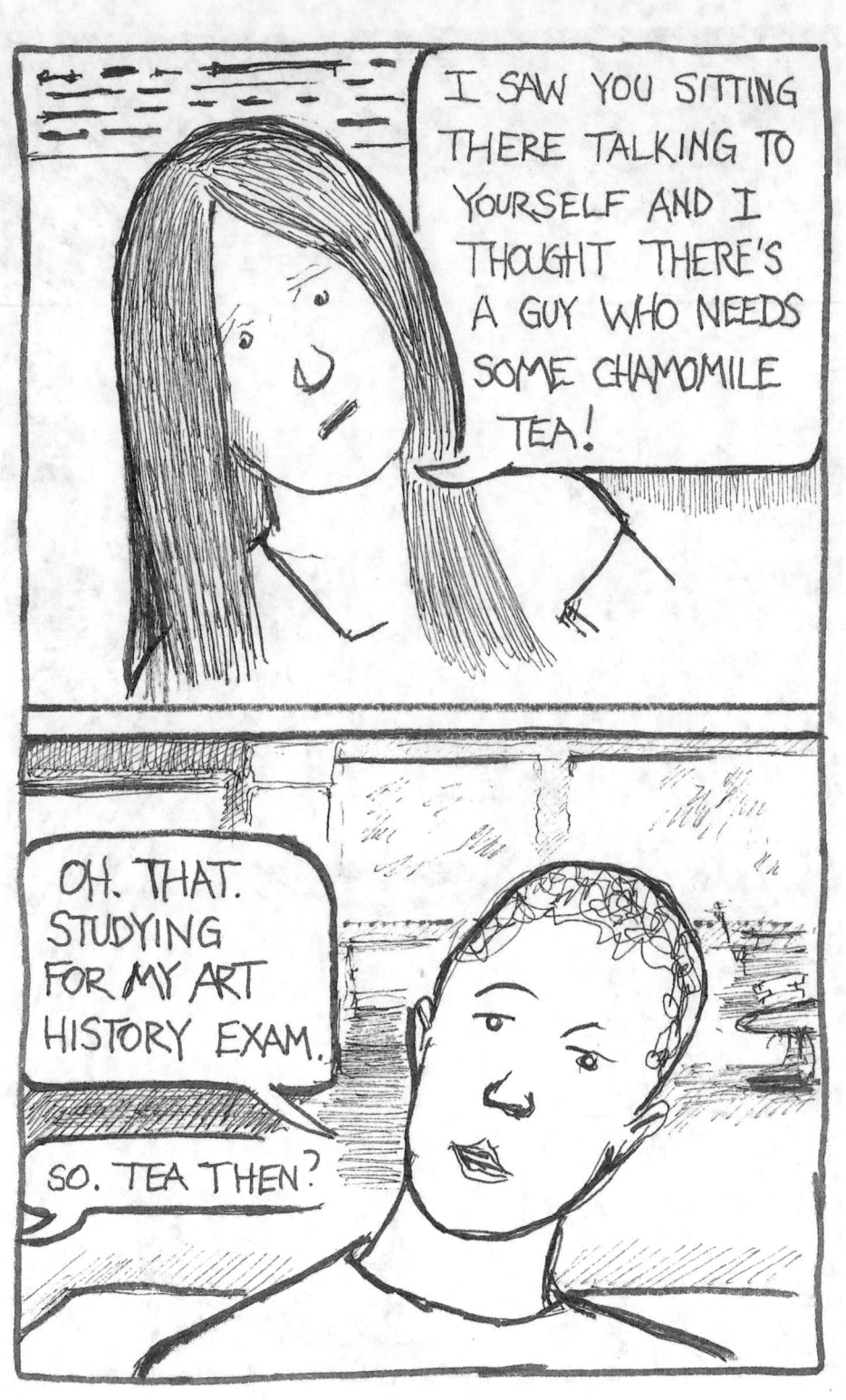

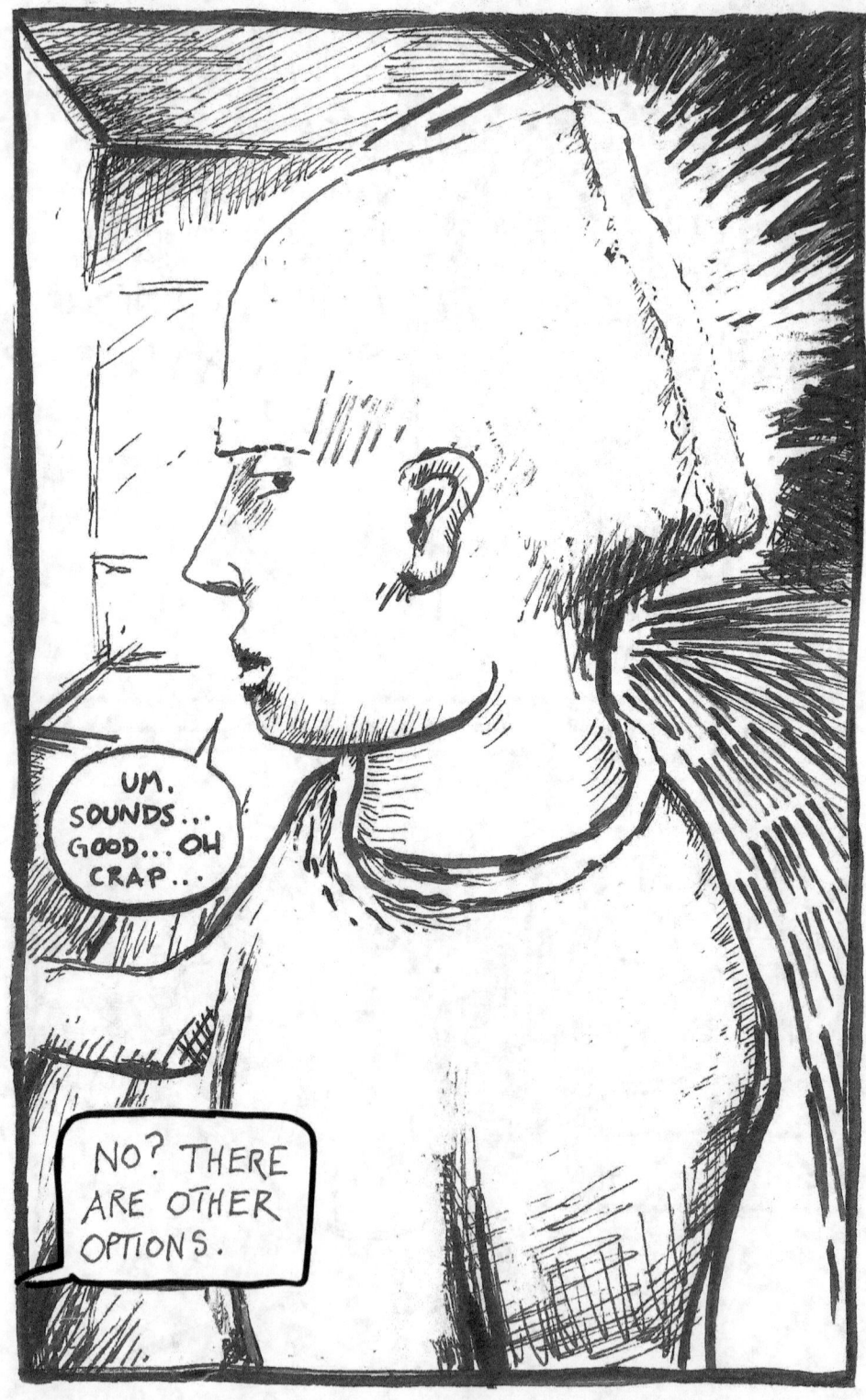

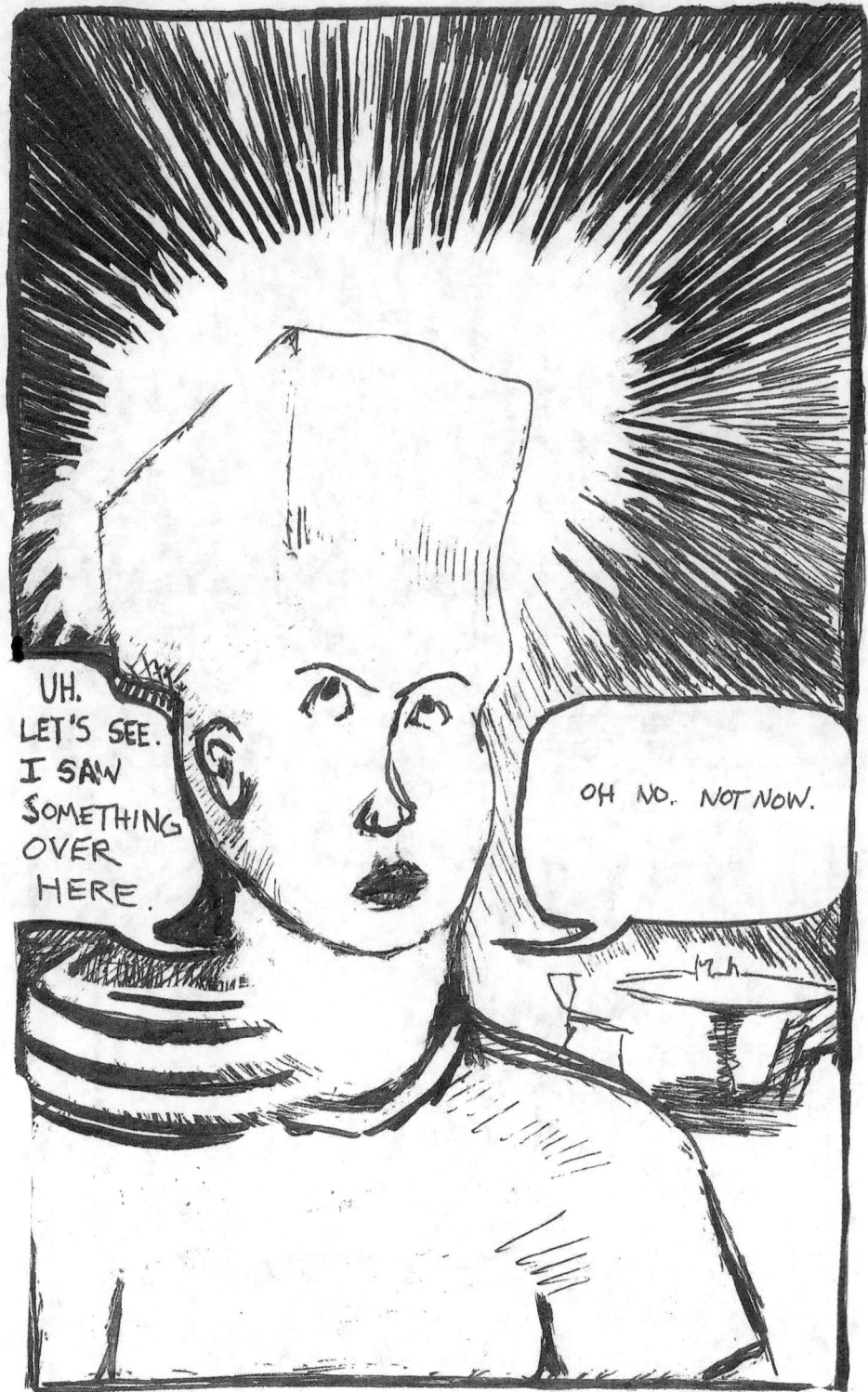

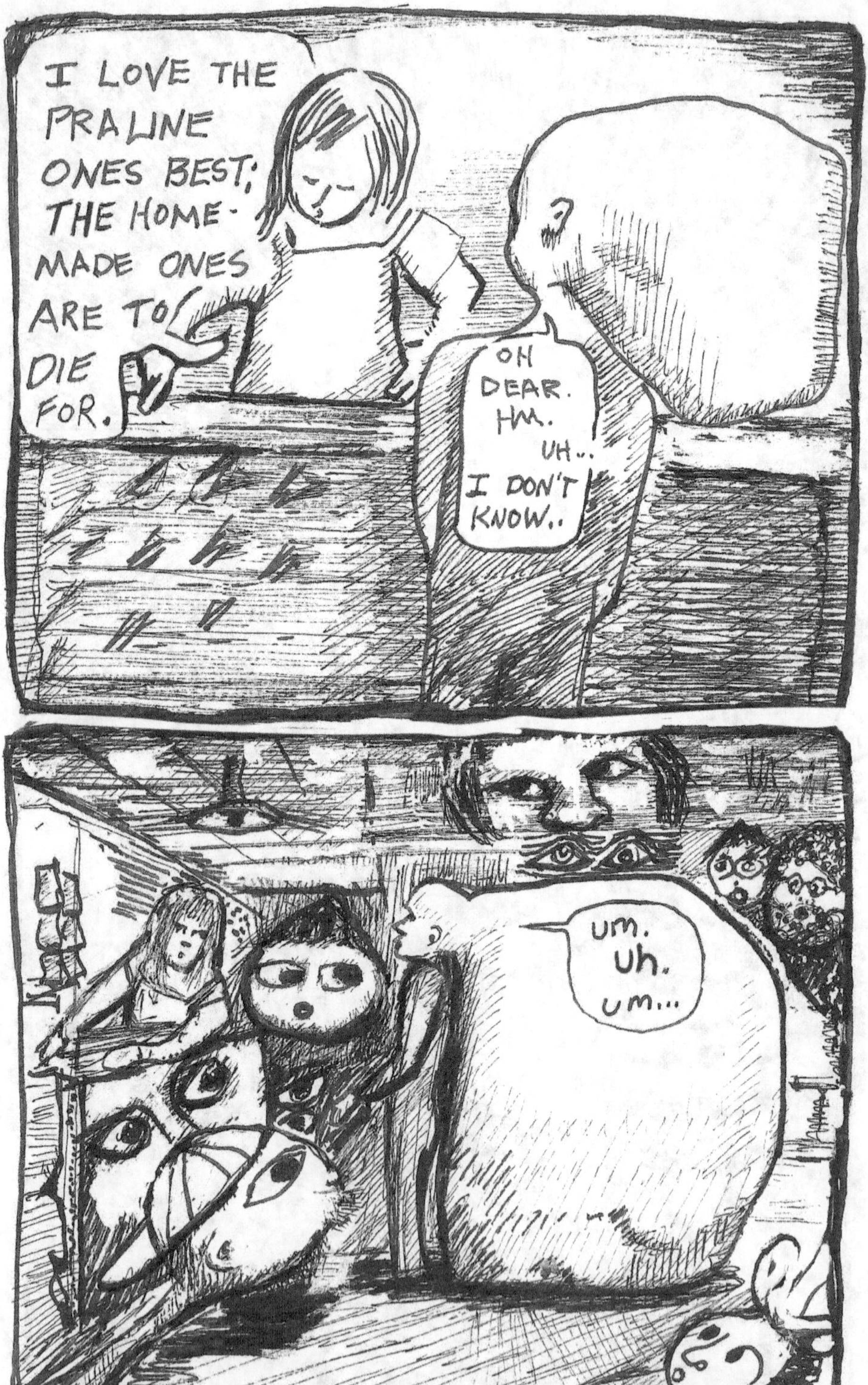
I LOVE THE PRALINE ONES BEST; THE HOME-MADE ONES ARE TO DIE FOR.
OH DEAR. HM. UH.. I DON'T KNOW..
um. Uh. um...

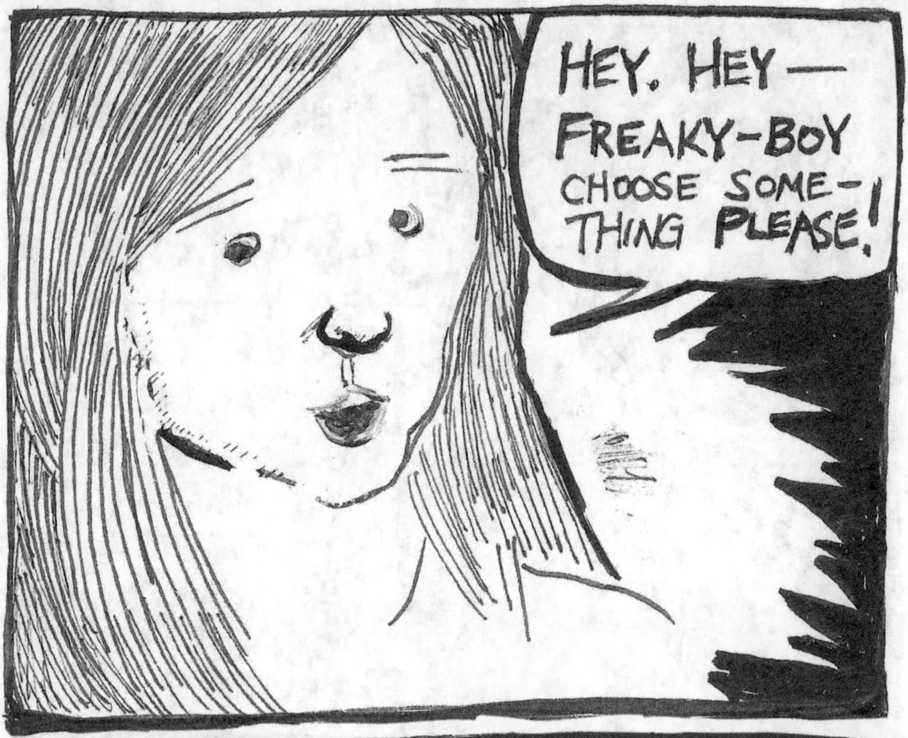
HEY. HEY— FREAKY-BOY CHOOSE SOME-THING PLEASE!

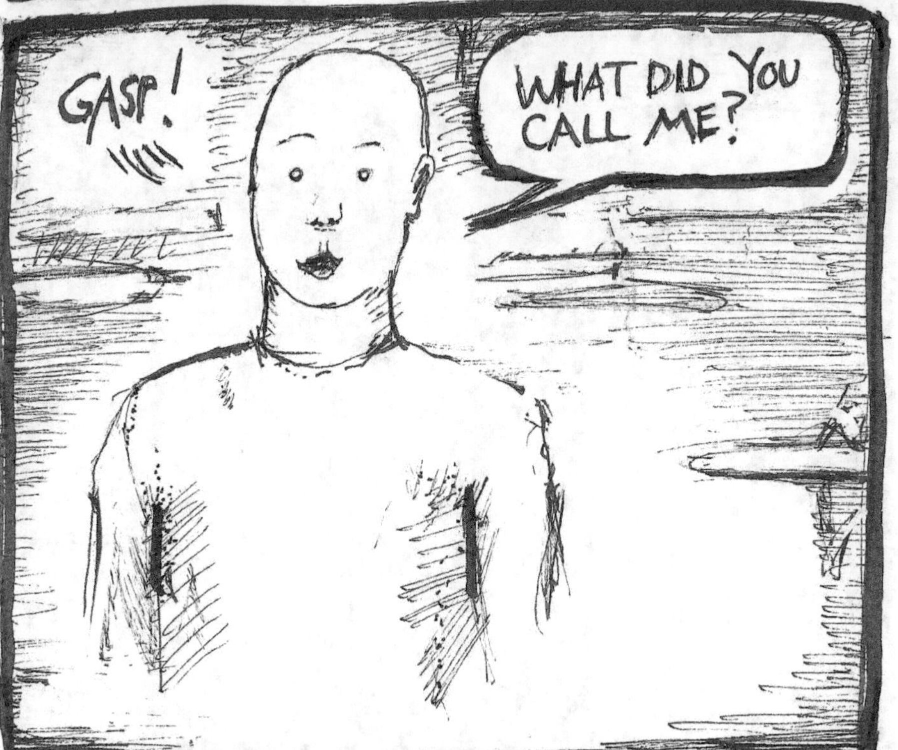
GASP!
WHAT DID YOU CALL ME?

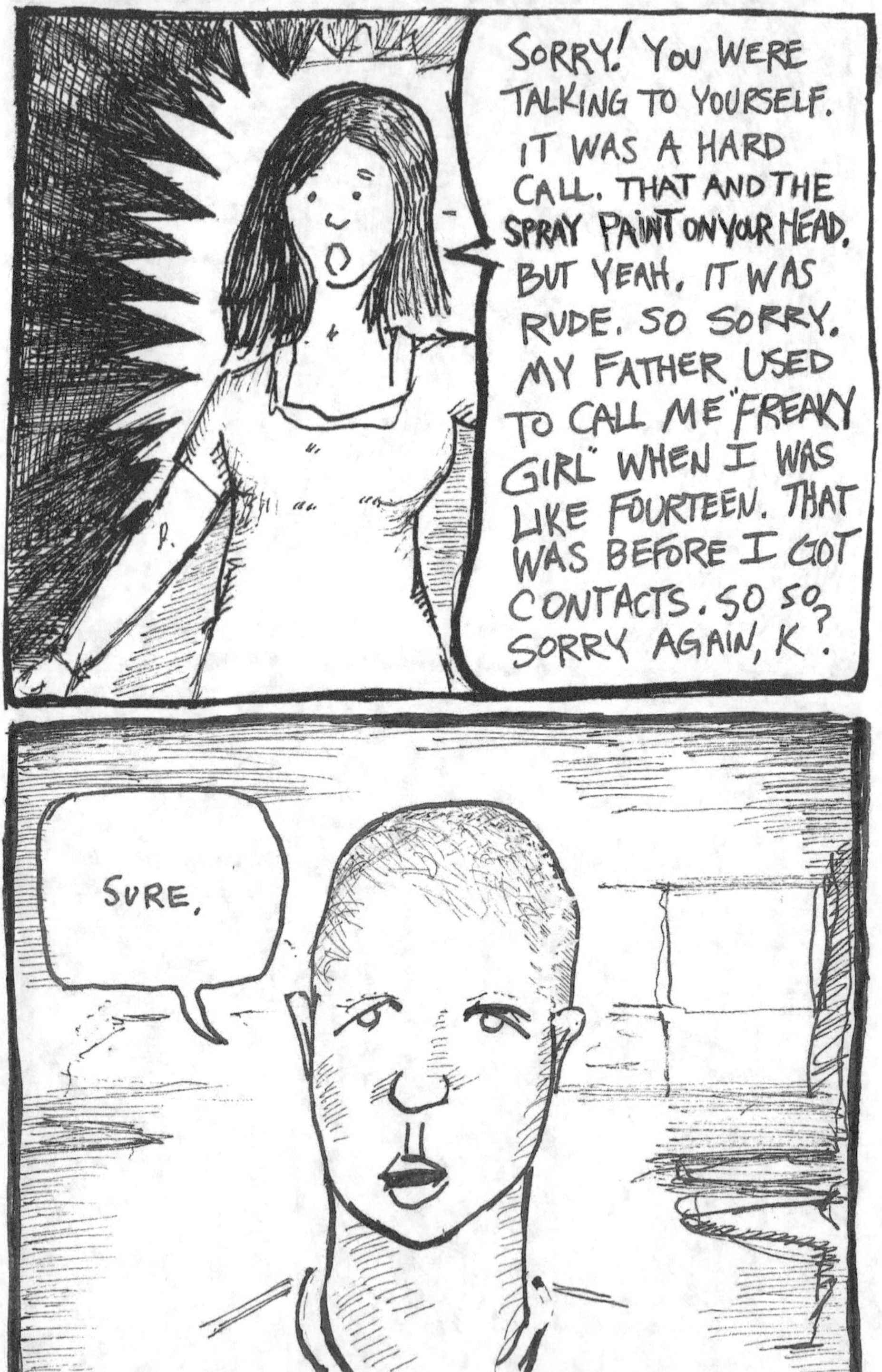
SORRY! YOU WERE TALKING TO YOURSELF. IT WAS A HARD CALL. THAT AND THE SPRAY PAINT ON YOUR HEAD. BUT YEAH, IT WAS RUDE. SO SORRY. MY FATHER USED TO CALL ME "FREAKY GIRL" WHEN I WAS LIKE FOURTEEN. THAT WAS BEFORE I GOT CONTACTS. SO SO SORRY AGAIN, K?
SURE.

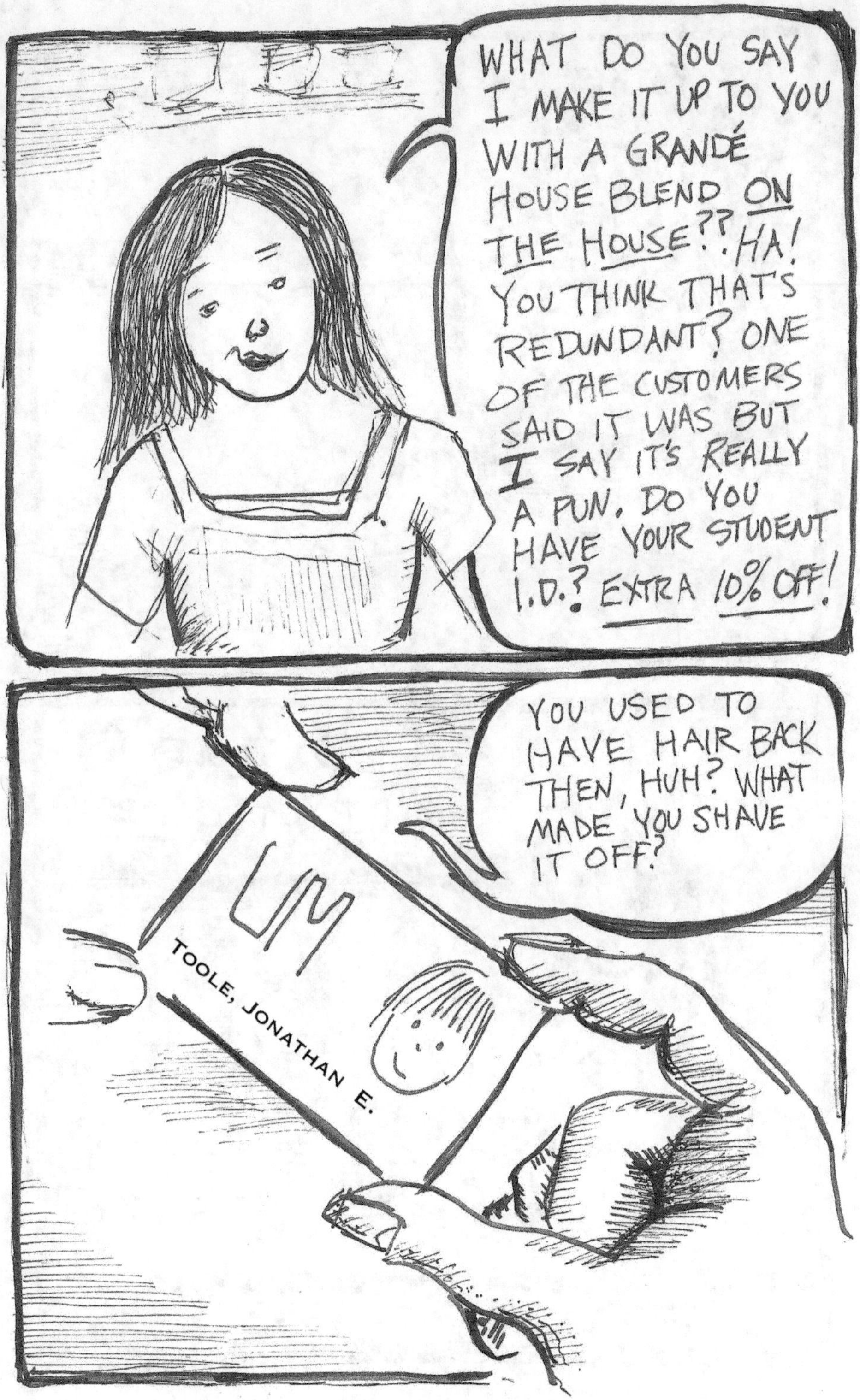
WHAT DO YOU SAY I MAKE IT UP TO YOU WITH A GRANDÉ HOUSE BLEND ON THE HOUSE?? HA! YOU THINK THAT'S REDUNDANT? ONE OF THE CUSTOMERS SAID IT WAS BUT I SAY IT'S REALLY A PUN. DO YOU HAVE YOUR STUDENT I.D.? EXTRA 10% OFF!
YOU USED TO HAVE HAIR BACK THEN, HUH? WHAT MADE YOU SHAVE IT OFF?
TOOLE, JONATHAN E.

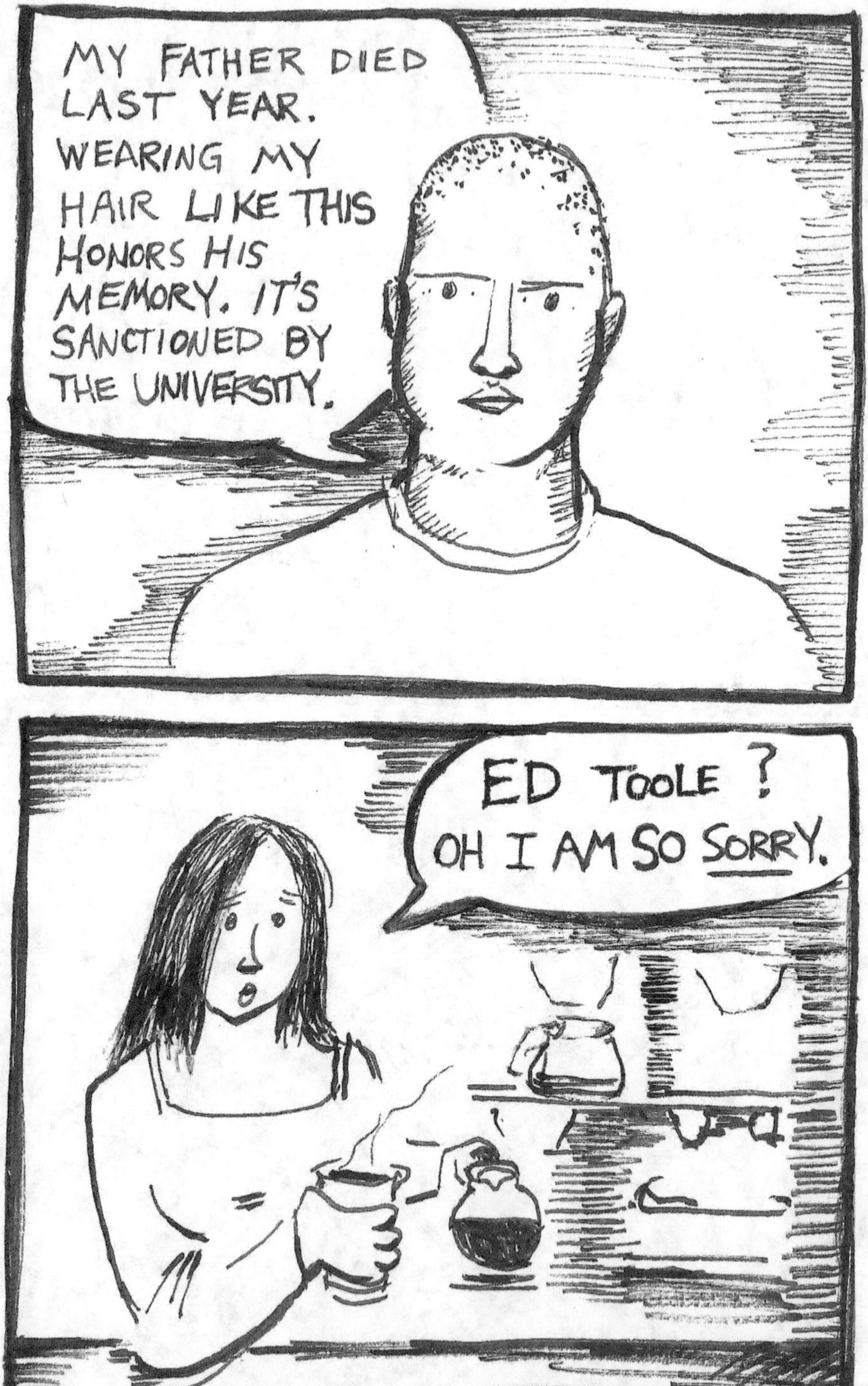

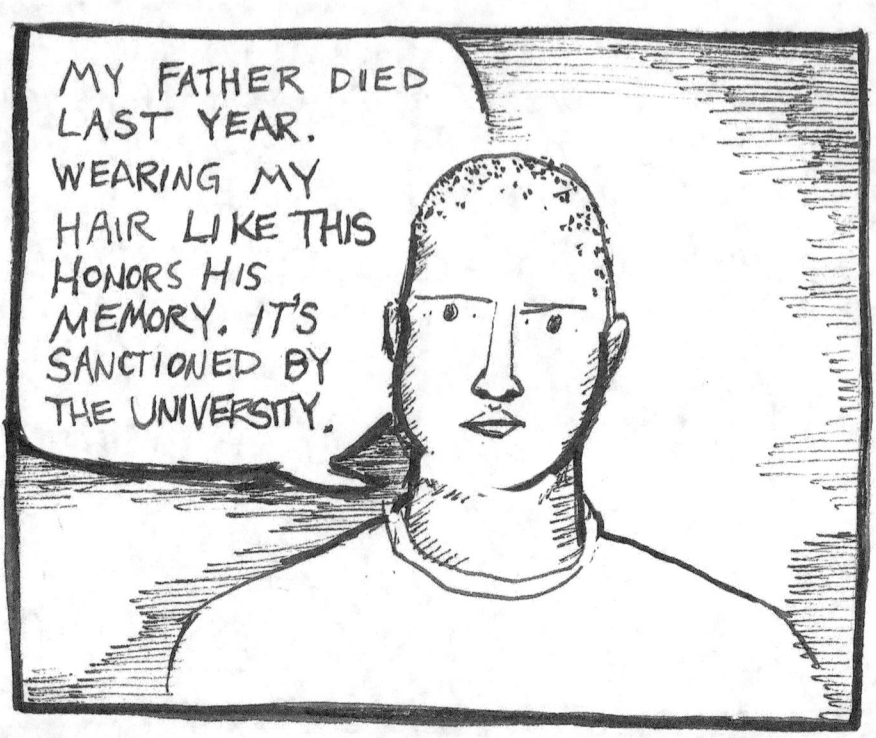

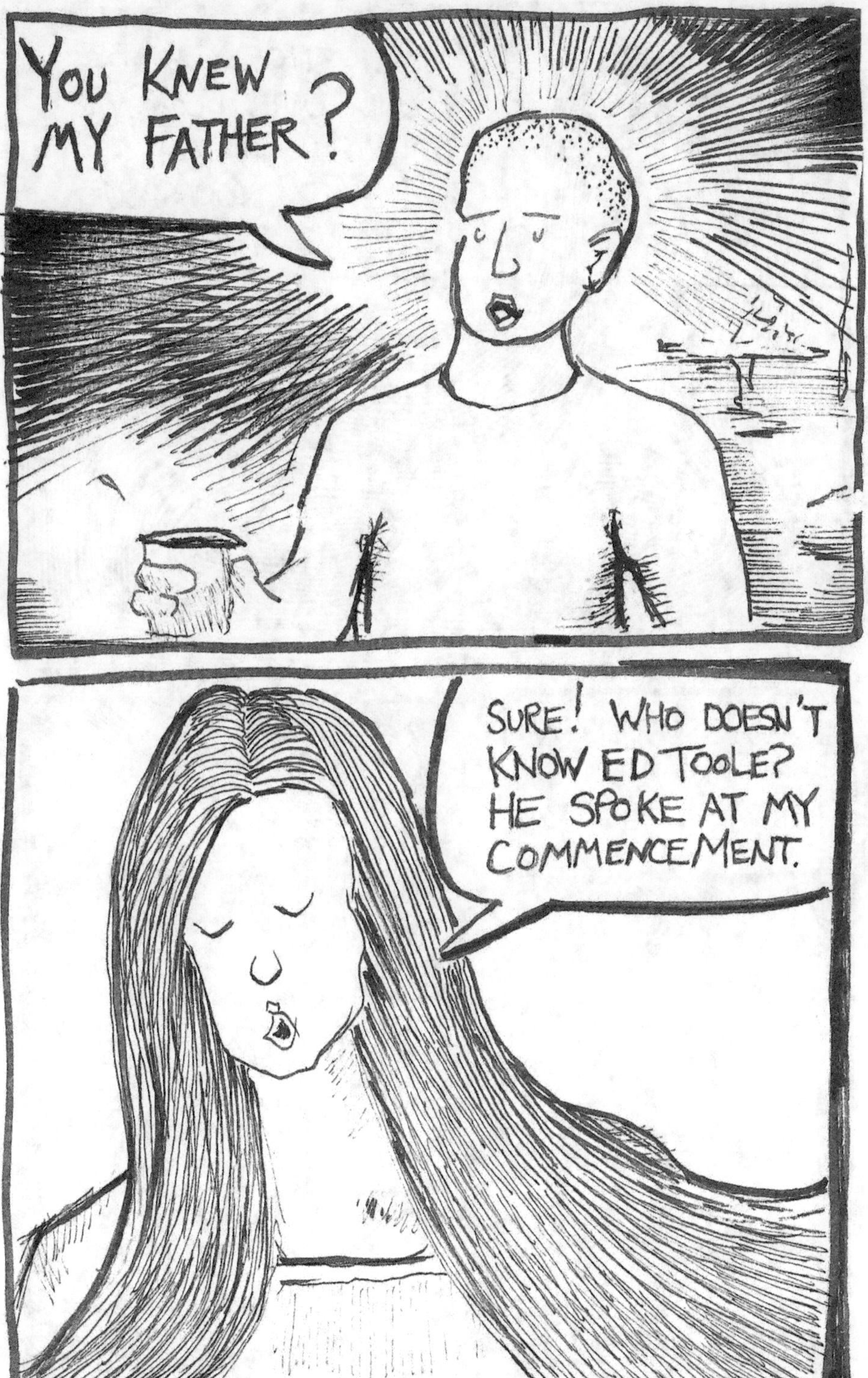
YOU KNEW MY FATHER?
SURE! WHO DOESN'T KNOW ED TOOLE? HE SPOKE AT MY COMMENCEMENT.

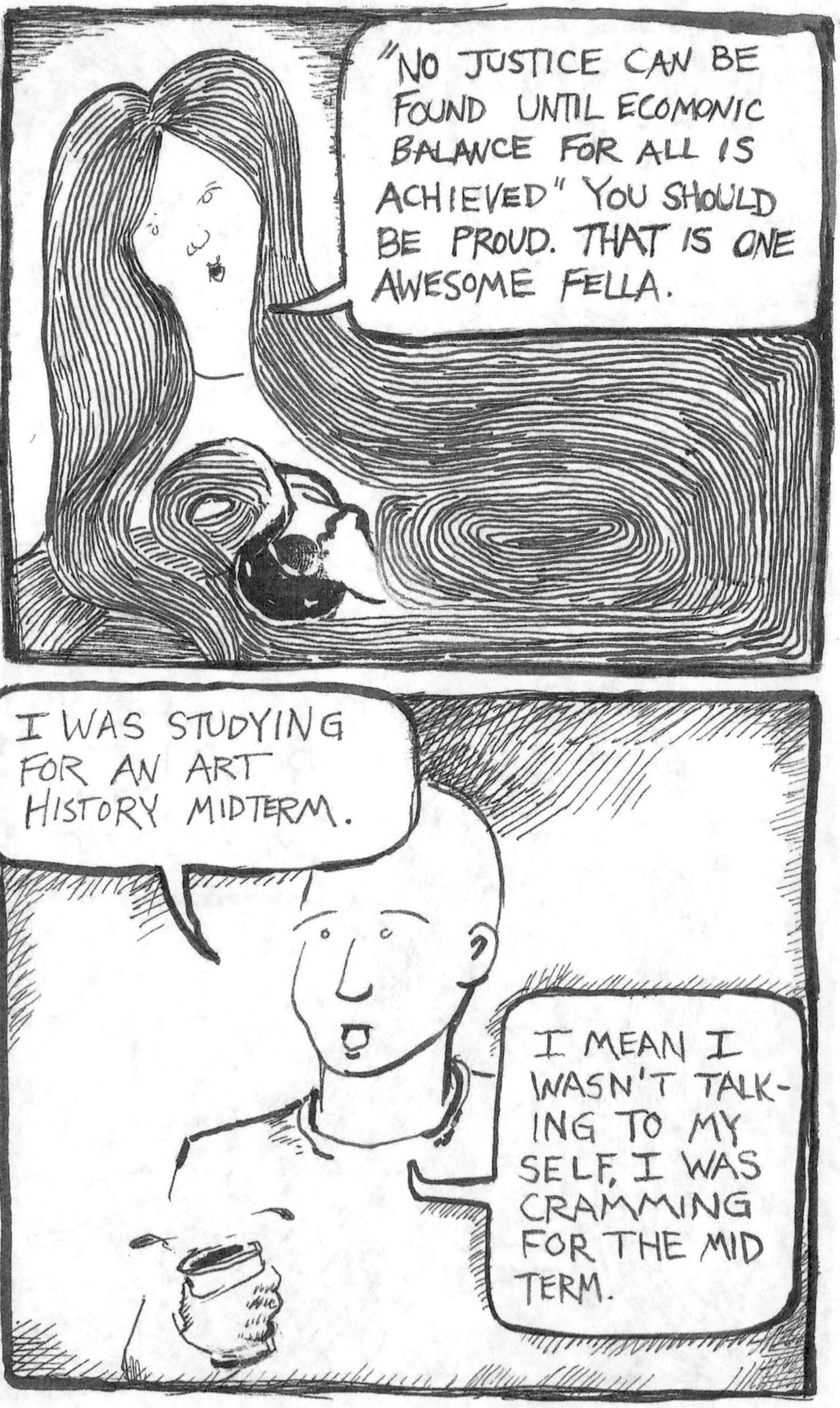
"NO JUSTICE CAN BE FOUND UNTIL ECOMONIC BALANCE FOR ALL IS ACHIEVED" YOU SHOULD BE PROUD. THAT IS ONE AWESOME FELLA.
I WAS STUDYING FOR AN ART HISTORY MIDTERM.
I MEAN I WASN'T TALK-ING TO MY SELF, I WAS CRAMMING FOR THE MID TERM.

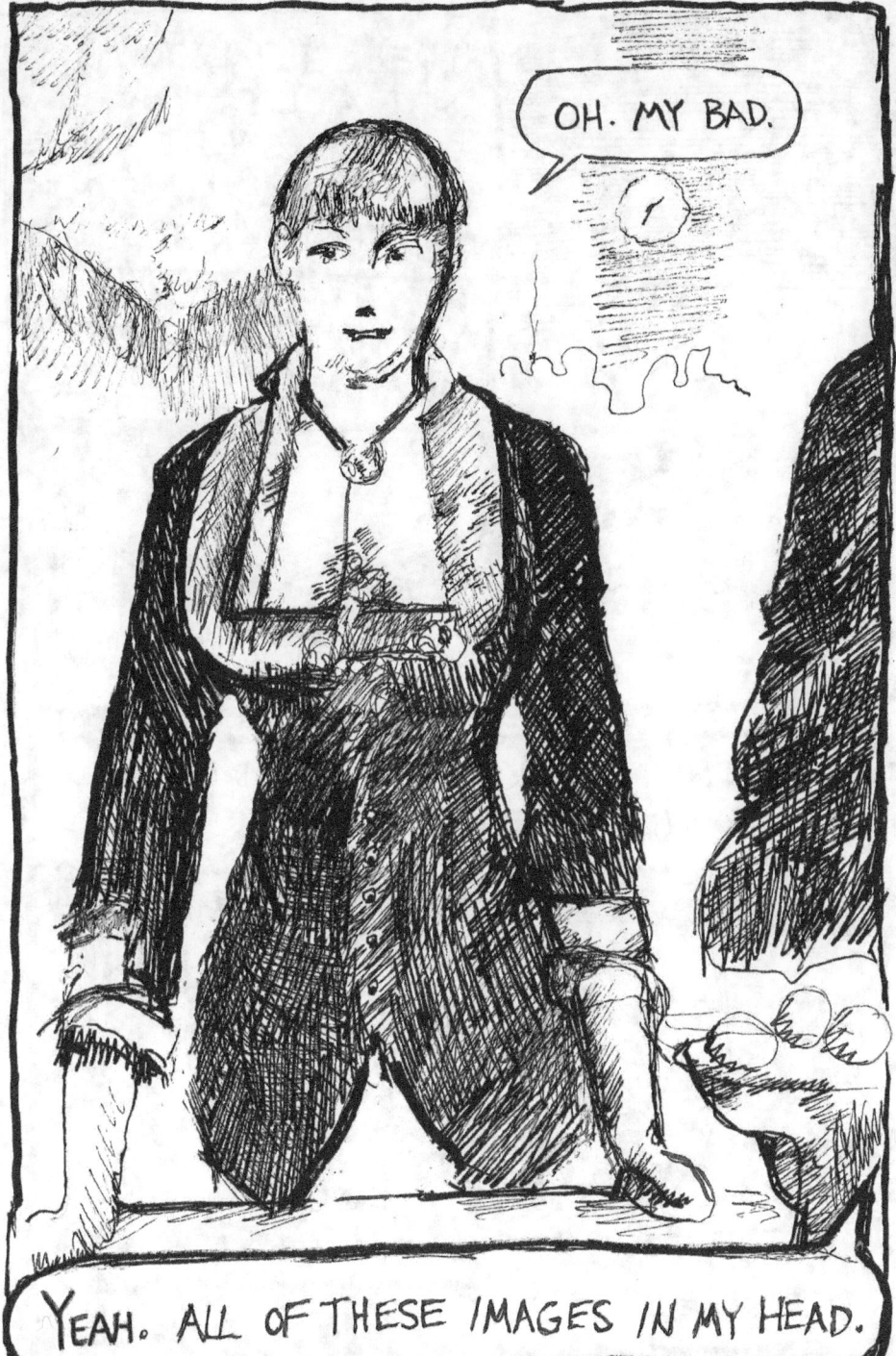

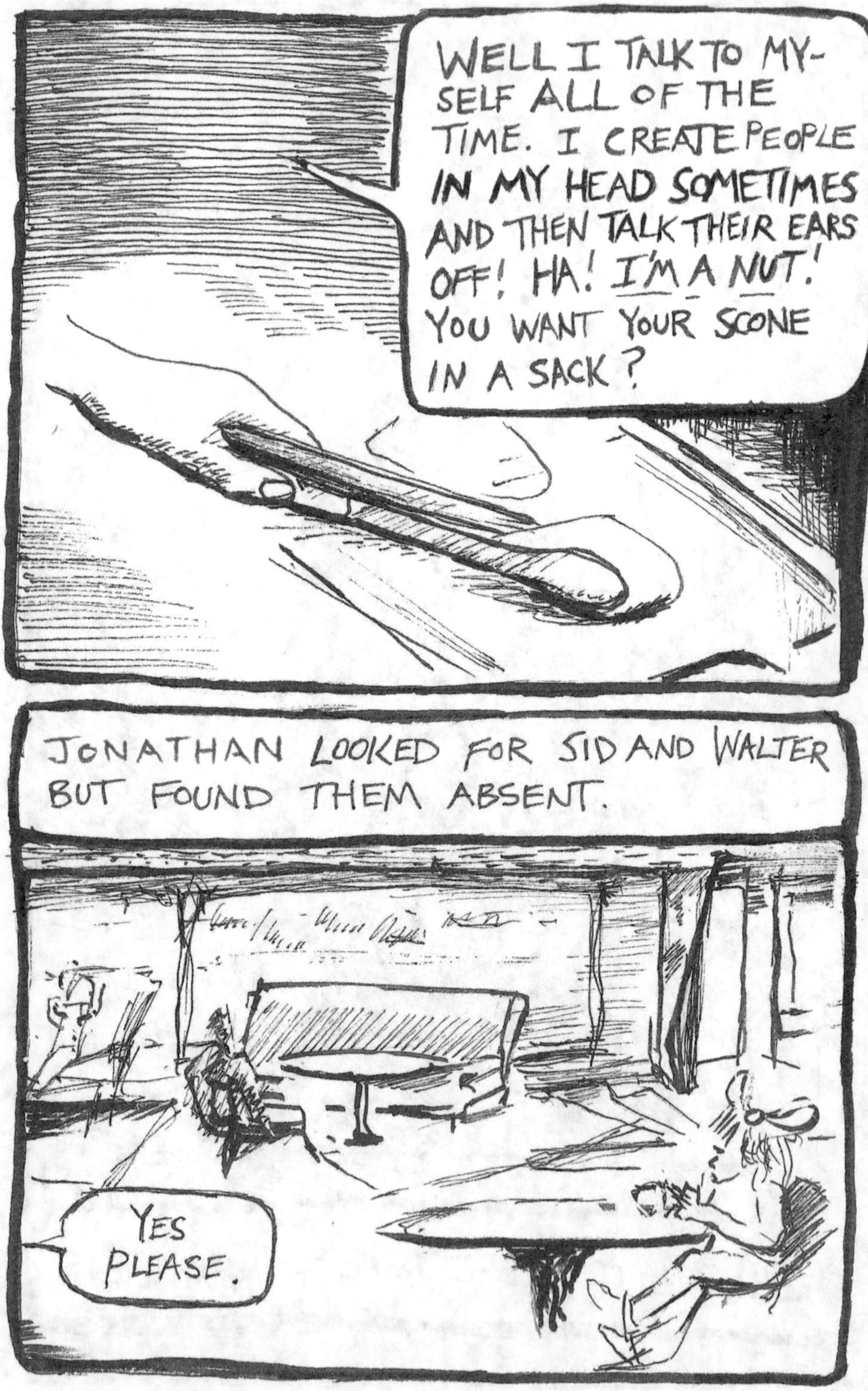

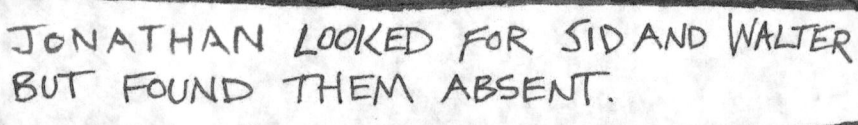

JONATHAN LOOKED FOR SID AND WALTER BUT FOUND THEM ABSENT.

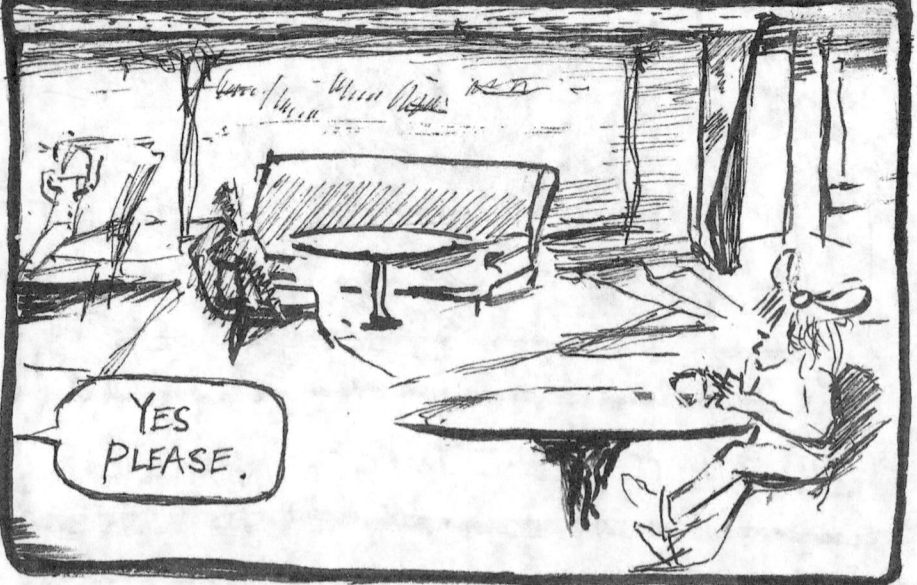

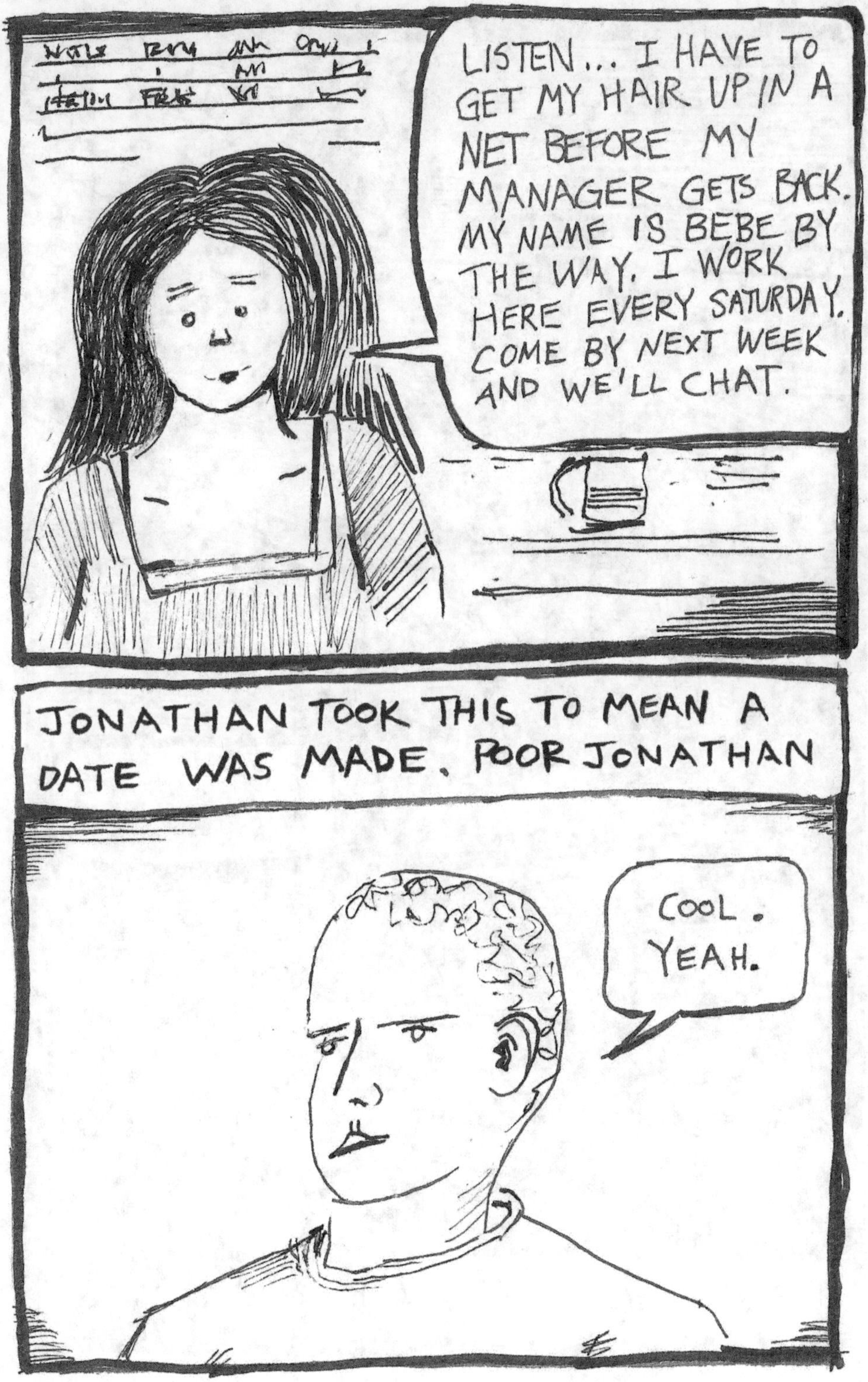
LISTEN... I HAVE TO GET MY HAIR UP IN A NET BEFORE MY MANAGER GETS BACK. MY NAME IS BEBE BY THE WAY. I WORK HERE EVERY SATURDAY. COME BY NEXT WEEK AND WE'LL CHAT.
JONATHAN TOOK THIS TO MEAN A DATE WAS MADE. POOR JONATHAN
COOL. YEAH.

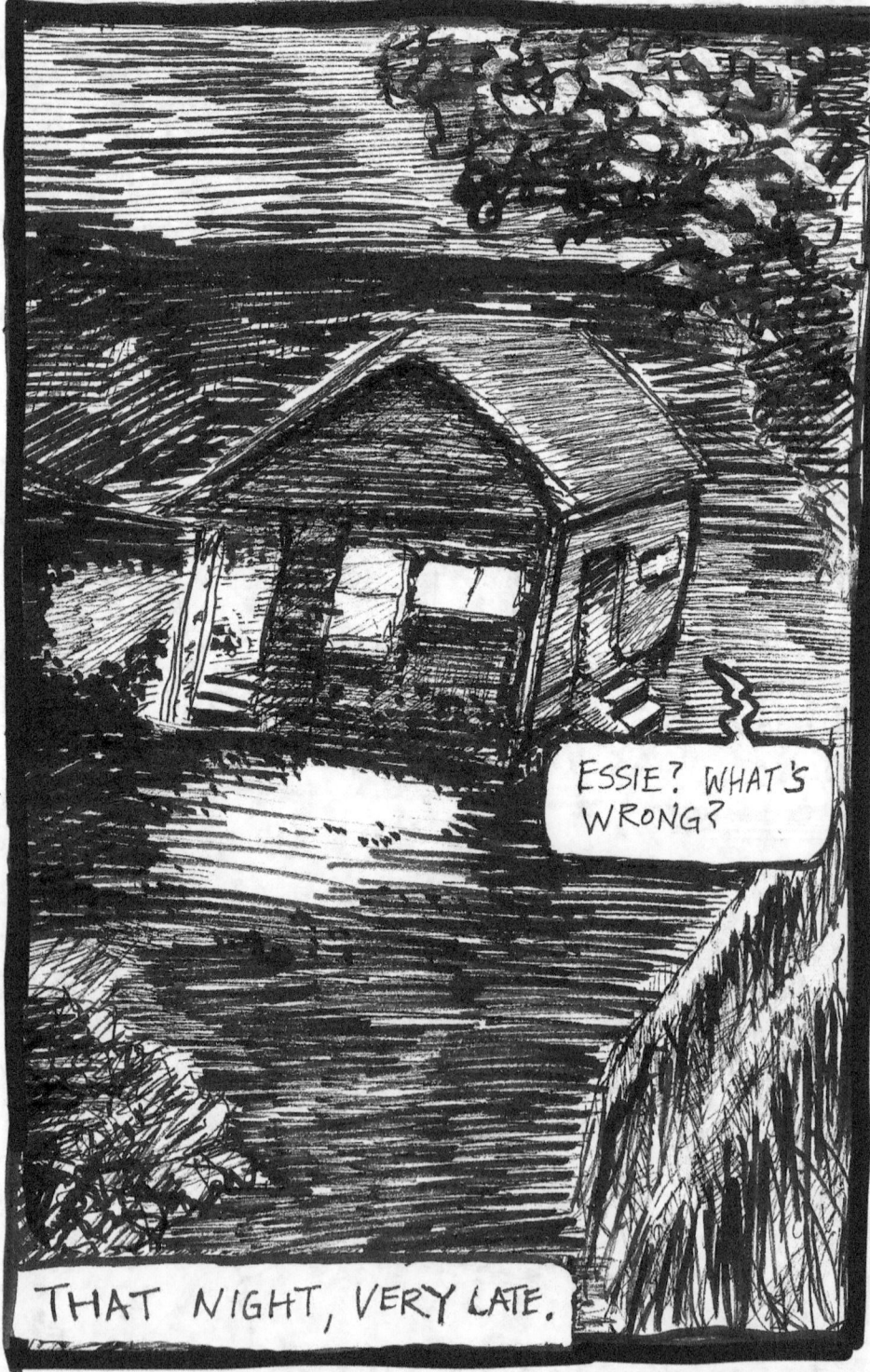

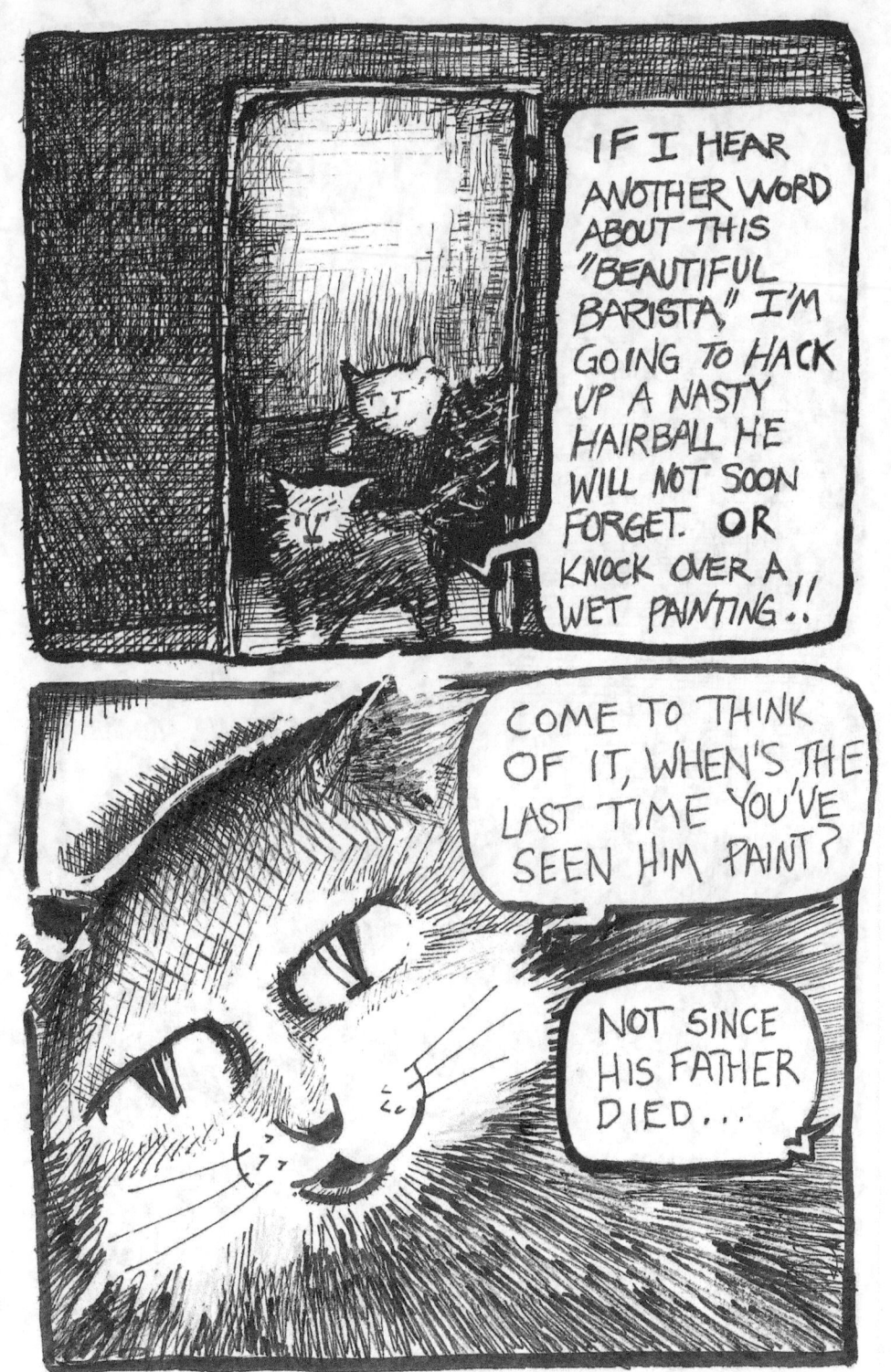

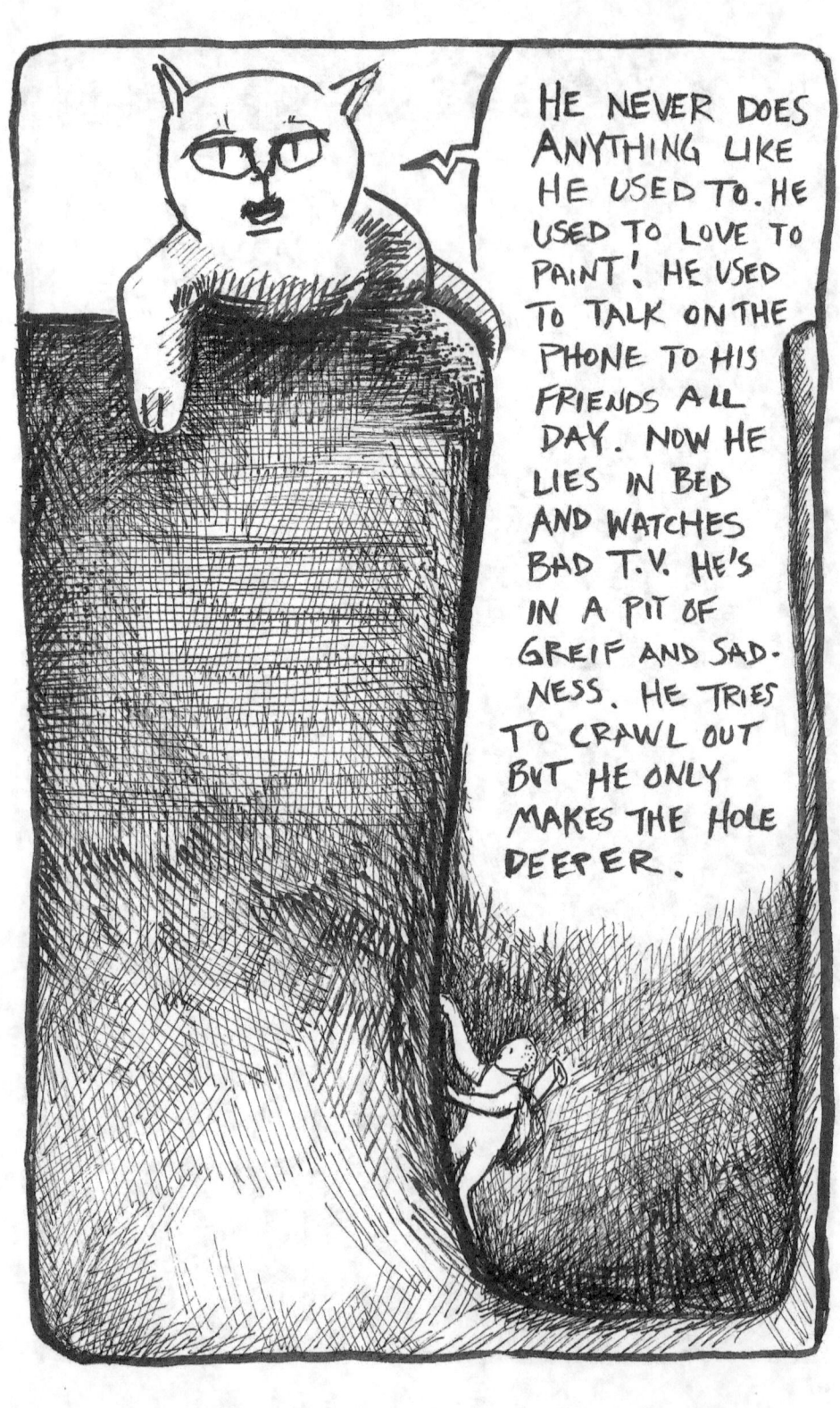

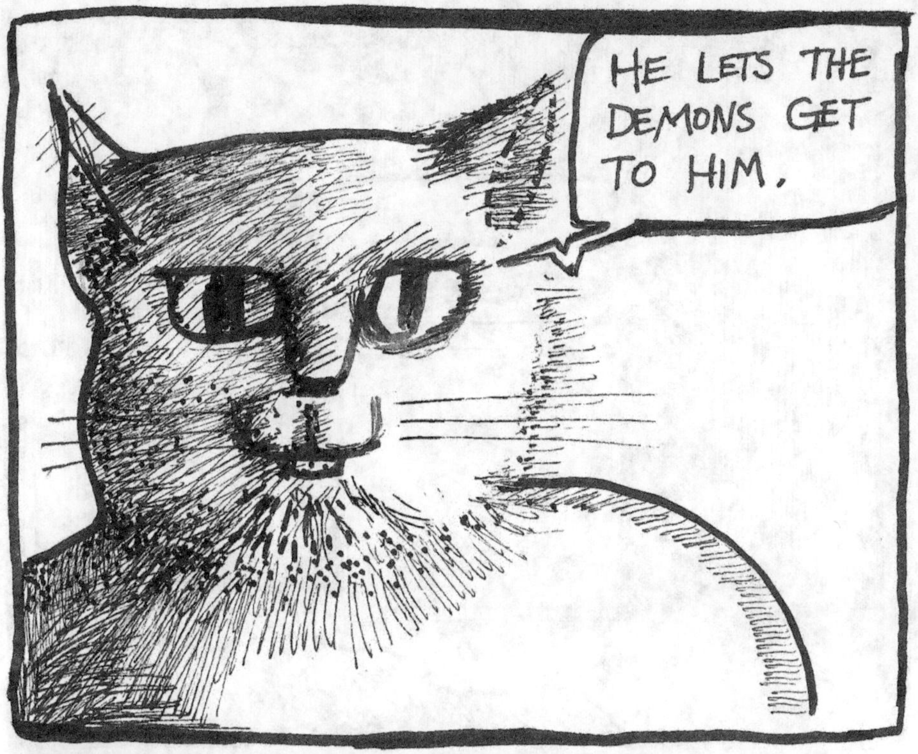
HE LETS THE DEMONS GET TO HIM.

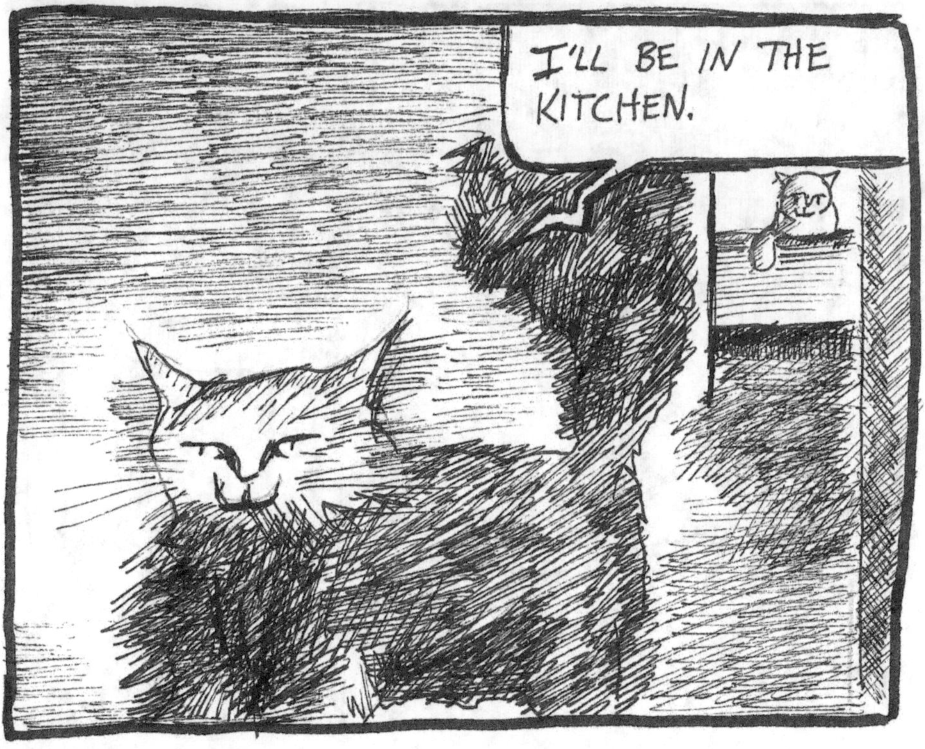
I'LL BE IN THE KITCHEN.

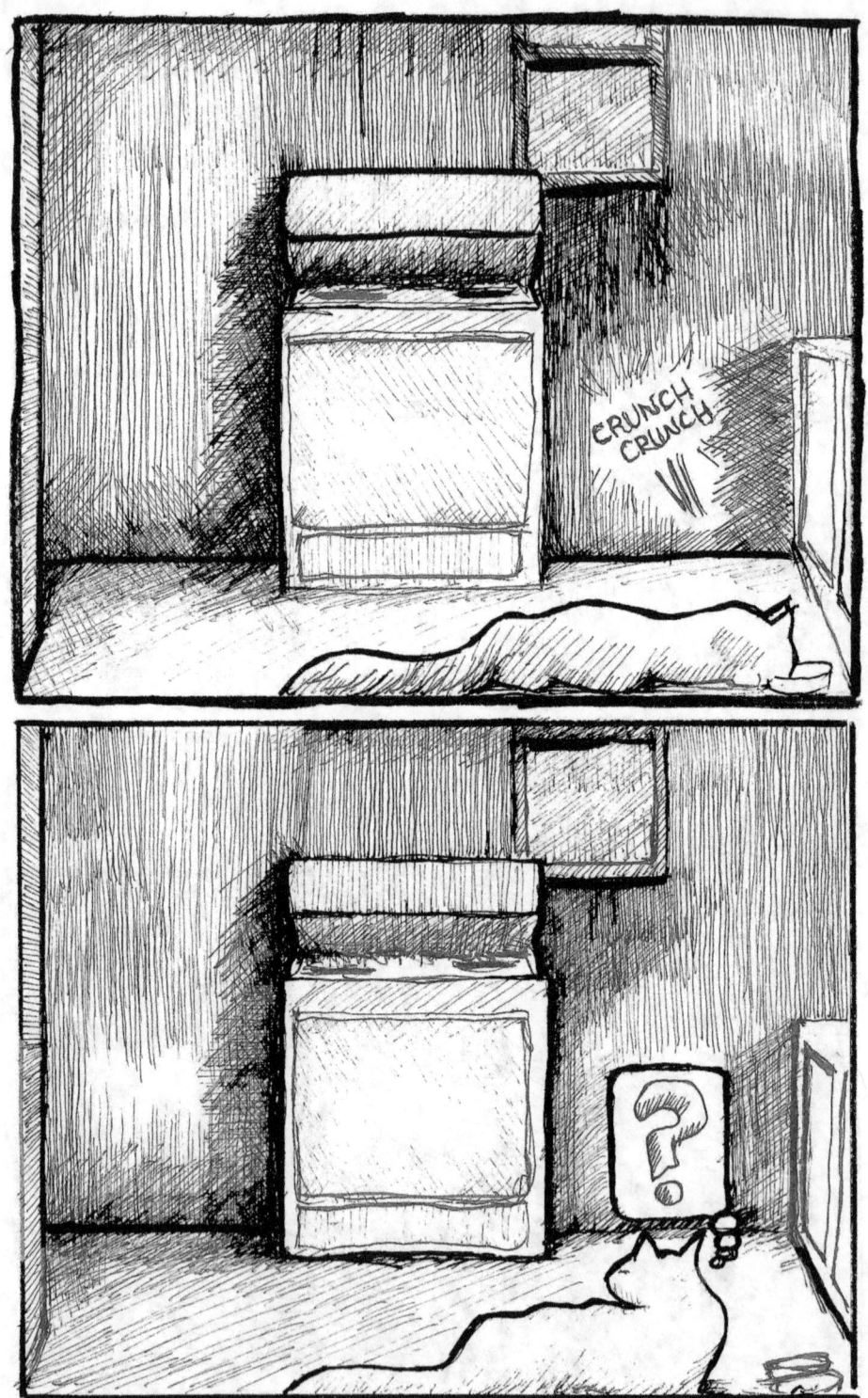

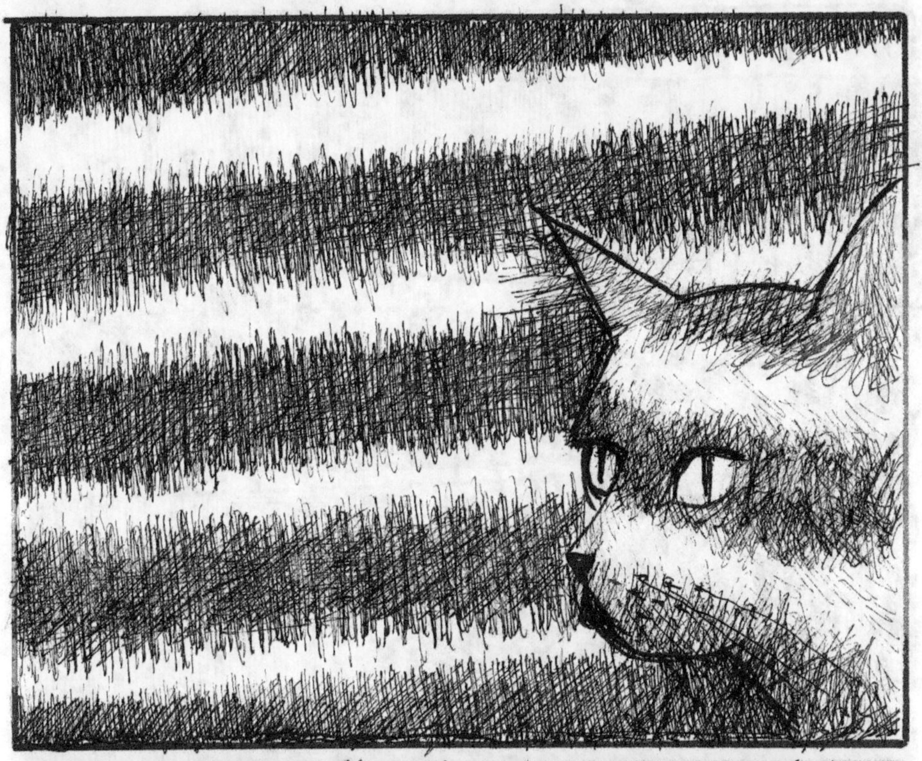

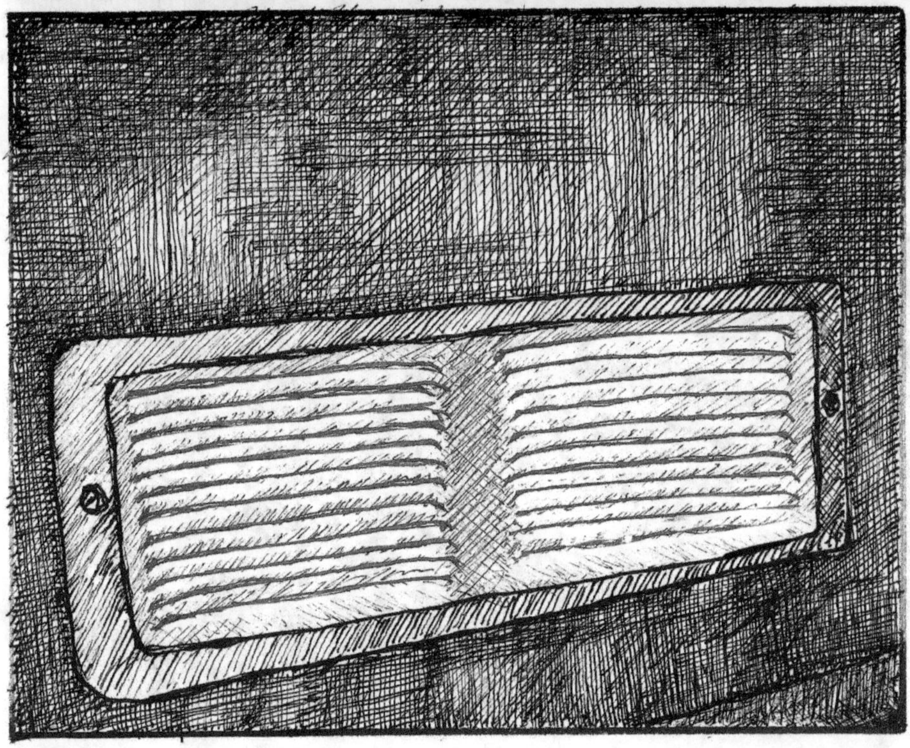

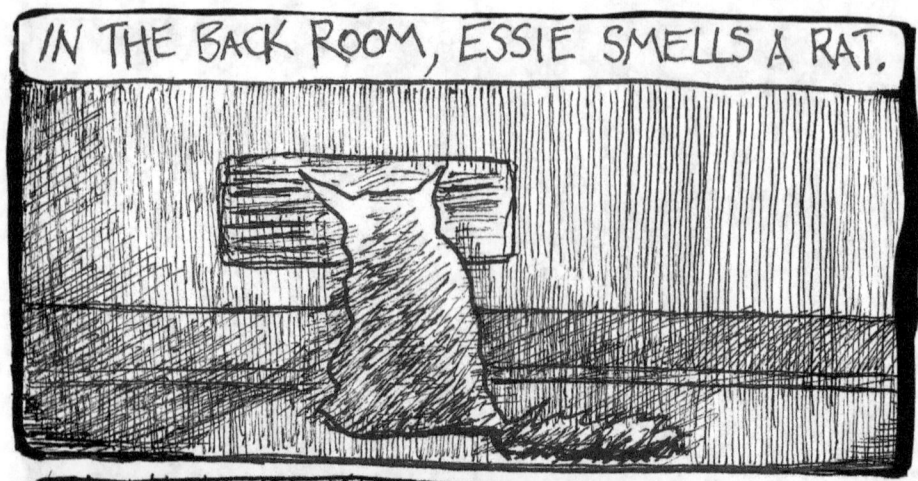

IN THE BACK ROOM, ESSIE SMELLS A RAT.

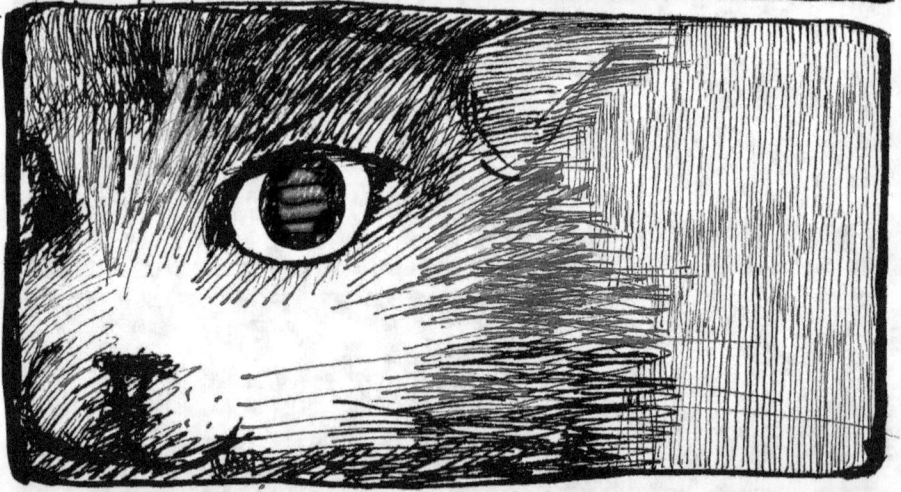

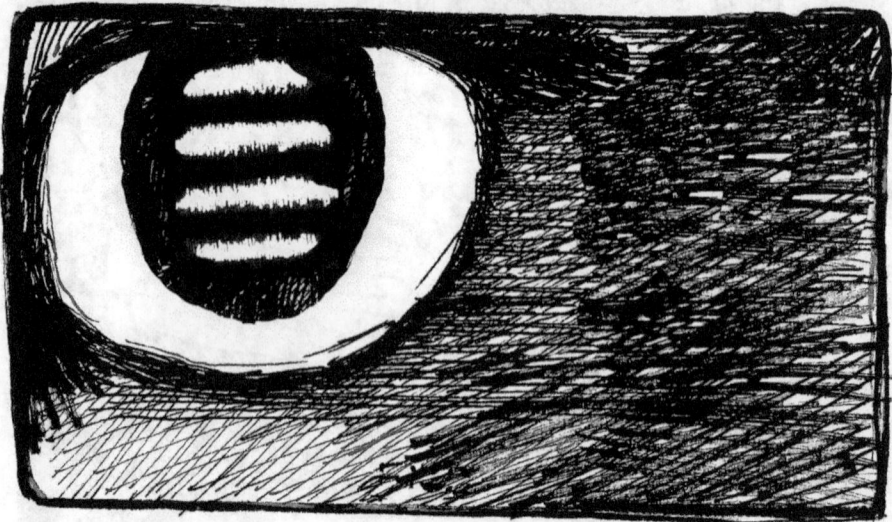

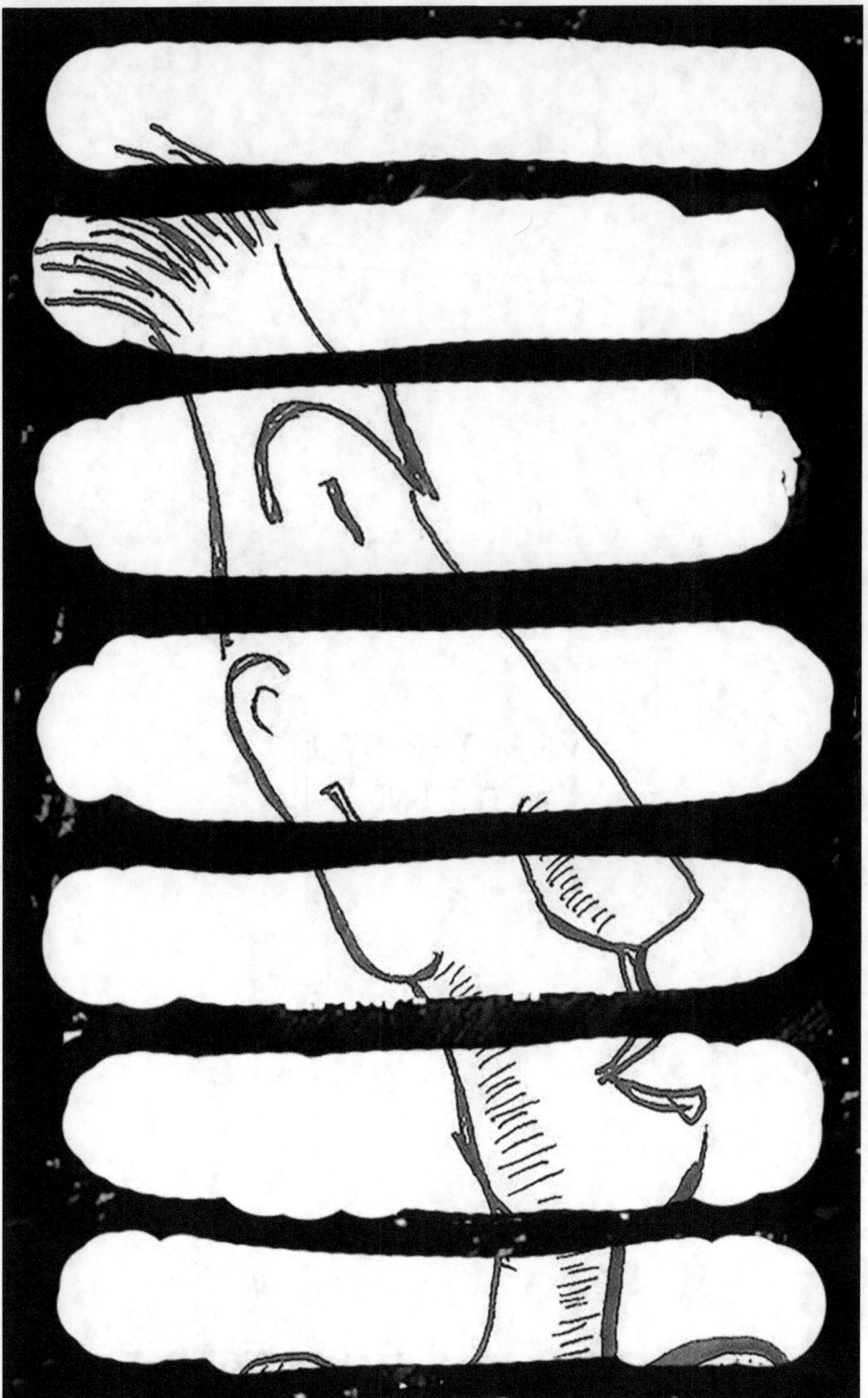

[CHAPTER TWO]
THE END

www.ingramcontent.com/pod-product-compliance
Lightning Source LLC
Chambersburg PA
CBHW062352290526
45794CB00005B/2193